The ISO 9000

Answer Book

Second Edition

ROB KANTNER

John Wiley & Sons, Inc.

New York • Chichester • Weinheim • Brisbane • Singapore • Toronto

This, the first of the rest,
is for Deanna—
whither thou goest.

This book is printed on acid-free paper. ⊚

Copyright © 2000 by Rob Kantner. All rights reserved.

Published by John Wiley & Sons, Inc.
Published simultaneously in Canada.

This publication is designed to provide accurate and authoritative information in regard
to the subject matter covered. It is sold with the understanding that the publisher is not
engaged in rendering legal, accounting, or other professional services. If legal advice or
other expert assistance is required, the services of a competent professional person should
be sought.

Library of Congress Cataloging-in-Publication Data:

Kantner, Rob.
      The ISO 9000 answer book / Robert Kantner. — 2nd ed.
          p. cm. — (Wiley quality management series)
      Includes bibliographical references and index.
      ISBN 0-471-35590-9 (alk. paper)
      1. ISO 9000 Series Standards.   I. Title.   II. Series.
   TS156.6.K36   2000
      658.5'62—dc21   99-052936

Printed in the United States of America.

10   9   8   7   6   5   4   3   2   1

Contents

PART TWO:
TECHNICAL REQUIREMENTS
AND GUIDELINES 27

PART THREE:
IMPLEMENTING—A
FIRST-TIMER'S GUIDE   183

Preface

It seems like a decade ago that I wrote the first edition of the book you hold in your hands. The writing of that book presented quite a challenge. The objective was to create a readable and easily understandable explanation of the content and implementation of ISO 9000: the international quality standard. Today's task is doubly difficult. ISO 9000: 2000 is a complete restructuring, and significant rewrite, of the earlier Standard. My goal is not only to create a readable and easily understandable explanation for newcomers but also a guide that can be used by *existing* registrants to plot and make their transition to the new Standard.

As with my earlier books, I have designed this to be a quick, easy-to-digest guide to the basics of the ISO 9000 process. It is aimed at management and supervisory people who may, up until now, have had little if any exposure to the "quality" disciplines. For that reason, I have tried to avoid using technical jargon and "quality-speak."

Throughout the writing of this book, I have incorporated comments and suggests from literally dozens of people—clients, friends, fellow consultants, and authorities of various kinds. But what I have drawn on most is my experience in helping clients of all sizes, shapes, and descriptions to implement quality systems that not only meet the requirements, and pass registration audits, but also help their firms to run better and improve their ability to meet customer needs.

That, to me, is what ISO 9000 is really all about. The 2000 revision, with its increased customer focus and process orientation, is a huge step in the right direction. I trust that you will find the information to be useful and helpful.

Whether you are already registered, or just getting started, there's plenty in here to help you. Welcome.

ACKNOWLEDGMENTS

I consider myself most fortunate in having had, as clients, only leaders and achievers. Even among this group, several stand out as unusually generous and gracious teachers and colleagues, and I thank them and all the rest for the continuing education: Michael Flanagan, Loren Hecker, Joe Kovacich, Jackie Smith, Tim Spina, Ellen Yoder, and Jay Zimmern.

Thanks also to Meaghan Kantner for her invaluable help.

ROB KANTNER

Plymouth, Michigan

How to Use This Book

This book is meant as a primer and a guide for two audiences:

1. People with little (if any) quality management orientation, working for organizations that are not involved in ISO 9000 yet.
2. People who work for registered firms that need to make the transition from ISO 900X: 1994 to ISO 9001: 2000.

The book is divided into four major sections. Each section has its own brief introduction. The book can be read in sequence (and considerable effort was made to present the information in logical order), but this is by no means necessary. I suspect that the majority of readers will use this book as a reference. I have, therefore, provided a complete contents, detailed index, and (most important) considerable amounts of cross-referencing within the chapters and sections. So feel free to hop, skip, and jump from topic to topic of interest.

Each of the 101 questions and answers includes:

- Detailed guidance.
- A capsule answer providing a snapshot of the guidance.
- Pitfalls and opportunities drawn from hands-on experience in implementing ISO 9000 in organizations of all kinds.

A great deal of time and study went into reading, pondering, and parsing ISO 9001: 2000 as it emerged from the word processors of TC/176 during the course of 1999. We relied on the DIS edition, published in December 1999; the "final" version, scheduled for November 2000, may vary. Where there were unclear points, guidance was sought and obtained by colleagues, friends, and other authorities.

Even so, ultimate interpretation of this new version of the Standard remains to be developed through field experience. We have tried our best to provide adequate direction in this book and have attempted to err on the side of conservatism. Any errors, omissions, or misinterpretations are truly honest ones for which we apologize in advance.

One last note: Reader feedback has been a tremendous help in the development of this book. Please feel free to send comments, questions, and suggestions to me at rob@9sg.com.

PART ONE

ISO 9000 Overview

1. What is ISO 9000?

CAPSULE ANSWER

ISO 9000 is a set of universally understood and accepted quality/ usiness practices which, when well implemented, give customers confidence that suppliers can consistently meet their needs.

ISO 9000 is a written set of rules (a "Standard") published by an international standards writing body (International Organization for Standardization—see Question 5). The rules define practices that are universally recognized and accepted for assuring that organizations consistently understand and meet the needs of their customers.

ISO 9000 is also highly generic. Its principles can be applied to any organization providing any product or service anywhere in the world.

Since meeting customer needs is one of the (many) definitions of quality, ISO 9000 is often called a quality system or a quality management system. But the rules, referred to as *requirements,* go beyond quality matters as they are traditionally understood. The requirements fall roughly into the following types:

- Requirements that help assure that the organization's output (whether product, service, or both) meets customer specifications. (Making, and keeping, them happy.)

- Requirements that assure that the quality system is consistently implemented and verifiable. (We must actually do what we say we are supposed to do. This must be verifiable via independent, objective audit.)
- Requirements for practices that measure the effectiveness of various aspects of the system. (In God we trust; all others bring data.)
- Requirements that support continuous improvement of the company's ability to meet customer needs. (We cannot sit still. We must strive to get better all the time, because customers change, and competitors gain strength.)

Nothing in ISO 9000 is new. The first edition, published by ISO in 1987, was drawn almost word for word from a British quality system standard. It in turn evolved from a long succession of written quality system specifications that had their ultimate origin in the defense and arms industries. Most of the practices required by ISO 9000 have been in use in industries of various kinds for decades. One intent of ISO 9000 is to simplify things for organizations. ISO 9000 strives to harmonize the sometimes conflicting, sometimes redundant quality programs that have traditionally been imposed by major corporations on their suppliers. (Note, however, that ISO 9000 is *not* meant to supersede customer, legal, or regulatory requirements.)

PITFALL

Organizations that implement ISO 9000 because they feel coerced—and therefore do a minimal and superficial job of it—end up with a system that adds only cost, not value.

Very often, major customers require or strongly "suggest" that their suppliers implement ISO 9000 systems. Equally often, such customers require independent verification that suppliers are meeting the requirements. So third-party registration bodies (Question 7) audit suppliers, confirm compliance to the ISO 9000 standard, and register the suppliers. It does not stop there. To stay registered, suppliers must undergo periodic (often semi-annual) surveillance audits, also carried out by their registration body.

Implementing an ISO 9000 quality system is neither cheap, nor easy. How costly and difficult it can be depends on:

- The level of commitment of senior management. (The single most important factor.)
- Where you are when you start. If you have already implemented a disciplined, documented quality system, you will have a less difficult time migrating to ISO 9000. (But that does not mean you will waltz to registration, either.)
- Whether your company (or any part of it) is "design responsible" or not (Question 13).
- How much time you have. If you are under the customer's gun and have merely months to get the job done, the process will be highly stressful.
- The physical size and configuration of your company.

The bottom line is this. ISO 9000 is a comprehensive set of rules—a business system, really—that can cause the way your organization runs to profoundly change, almost always for the better. Yet, because it is often customer-mandated, many suppliers regard ISO 9000 as "just another hoop to jump through to keep our customers happy." They see their choice as swallow hard, pony up, and jump through the hoops; or walk away from the customer.

What many do not fully appreciate is that implementing ISO 9000—expensive, exhausting, and annoying as it can be—can also have the salutary effect of improving the performance of your organization. Not just at first, but on an ongoing basis.

2. What is the goal and scope of an ISO 9000 quality system?

CAPSULE ANSWER

The goal of the Standard is customer satisfaction. Its scope is universal.

The Standard states its goal in two blunt words: *customer satisfaction*. How do we achieve customer satisfaction? By meeting customer requirements. The quality management system (QMS) helps us to do this by:

- *Applying the system*. Actually using it. Putting it at the heart of our organization.
- *Continually improving the system*. The QMS is never done. After all, customer requirements do not stand still—they evolve and

grow tougher. So we have to *improve* continually in order to survive. (The guidance document, ISO 9004: 2000, sets a compatible and in some respects more ambitious goal: "improving the processes of an organization to enhance performance.")

■ *Prevention of nonconformity.* Prevention is the key term here: prevention, rather than detection. Quality management has long since evolved away from the old "inspect quality in" approach. *Prevention* is cheaper, more effective, and more protective of the customer. Detection is also a different mindset. It requires a very high degree of process orientation, upstream thinking, and relentless analysis.

OPPORTUNITY

Many think of ISO 9000 as applying only to manufacturing firms. But ISO 9000 has been implemented in law offices, colleges, trading firms, and hospitals.

To what types of organizations does the Standard apply? All types. The requirements "are generic and applicable to all organizations, regardless of type and size." A compliant QMS can be implemented by any organization, producing any product or service, anywhere in the world.

Within the organization, the impact of the requirements and the QMS are similarly broad. The Standard "applies to the activities of organizations from the identification of customer requirements, through all quality management system processes, to the achievement of customer satisfaction." Every activity within the organization that impacts the process of creating customer satisfaction is affected by the requirements of the Standard.

3. Why do organizations implement ISO 9000 systems?

CAPSULE ANSWER

Many implement because of customer pressure. Others implement to improve their operations.

More often than not, organizations get ISO 9000 because certain customers force them or encourage them to.

In many market sectors—electronics, pulp and paper, telecommunications, automobile manufacturing, defense—major customers have mandated ISO 9000 registration to their key suppliers. Similarly, some overseas regulatory bodies mandate ISO 9000 for the makers of quality-sensitive products (such as medical devices).

Many of these major customers impose ISO 9000 systems *in place of, or in addition to,* specific quality programs, requirements, specifications, and so on that have been in place for many years. The ISO 9000 Standard becomes a key part of the relationship between the customer and its suppliers.

ISO 9000 is not, however, meant to replace customer-specific requirements in any market segment. Rather, ISO 9000 is meant to be a *floor:* a basic set of generic requirements. They are generic enough to apply to virtually all supplier/customer relationships anywhere in the world. It matters not the size of the supplier, the location of the customer, or the nationalities involved.

In some industrial segments, formalized standards have been created, adding to the generic ISO 9000 requirements additional clauses that are industry specific. Examples include:

- Automotive (QS-9000).
- Aerospace (AS-9000).
- Telecommunications (TL-9000).

To the extent that ISO 9000 replaces customer-specific quality programs and supporting audit/oversight activities, it can relieve both customers and suppliers of a great deal of redundancy, duplication, and waste of resources. The fundamental requirements are understood, agreed to, and (usually) confirmed by objective third-party audit. This gives customers confidence in the integrity and effectiveness of their supplier's basic quality practices. The customer and supplier can then

OPPORTUNITY

If your organization works to a documented quality system of any kind, this can be an ideal springboard for implementing ISO 9000. There is no need to reinvent the wheel.

invest their energies and resources in agreeing to and working on the specific requirements unique to their relationship.

To some, ISO 9000 sounds like a mandatory, gun-to-your-head, my-way-or-the-highway program. For many suppliers, it is exactly that ("get ISO 9000 or get lost"). For many others, it is perceived that way: "They're trying to tell us how to run our businesses."

But the goal of ISO 9000 is not to strengthen customers' control over how their suppliers run their businesses. The goal is to give customers confidence in the ability of suppliers to meet their needs, resulting in satisfied customers, and growing and prosperous suppliers.

Admittedly, implementing ISO 9000 does not guarantee this. Like most things, what you get out of it depends on what you put into it. You can implement a compliant ISO 9000 system that is all cost and no benefit and it's even possible to pass registration audit (Question 95) this way. This happens, usually, when the supplier's approach is to try to:

- Squeak by.
- Do just enough to get registered.
- Get this thing done without changing how we work.

But suppliers who implement ISO 9000 fully—to the spirit, as well as the letter—can and do achieve real benefits.

4. What are the advantages or benefits of implementing an ISO 9000 quality system?

CAPSULE ANSWER

An ISO 9000 system unites the organization in a well-defined, continually improving process that meets customer needs.

If you get into ISO 9000 just to pacify customers (Question 3)—and do not pursue it for the other benefits it provides—you are setting yourself up to be in the worst possible position: ISO 9000 as a cost, rather than as a benefit.

What can a well-implemented ISO 9000 system do for you?

- *Improves customer focus and process orientation within the organization.* A well-implemented, well-understood system helps all functions within the process to understand their responsibility for meeting customer needs, and appreciate their position in the overall process for doing so.
- *Facilitates continuous improvement.* The requirements are saturated with admonitions to monitor, review, and improve the subprocesses of the quality system. There is even a direct requirement that the quality management system be continually improved (Question 17). The corrective and preventive action activities required by the Standard enlist all levels and functions in the effort to prevent quality problems and quickly mitigate those that do occur.
- *Creates consistency throughout the organization.* It establishes and enforces consistent working methods and quality controls throughout the organization. This can be especially important in larger, multisite organizations whose facilities are major suppliers to each other.
- *Strengthens relationships* between your organization and its suppliers and customers, and among suppliers/customers within your organization. A documented quality system, especially in light of ISO 9000's process orientation, is common ground for addressing quality issues of mutual importance.
- *Provides confidence* to customers in the capability of your organization to meet quality commitments. This benefit is much stronger when the quality system is registered.
- *Improves management decision making.* A quality system is an information system. Internal audits, management reviews, analysis of organization-level data, and effective document and data control—four strong pillars of ISO 9000—provide management with the intelligence it needs to make the right moves.
- *Institutionalizes training* in methods and procedures essential to quality.
- *Reduces dependence upon individuals.* People are vital to quality, but people also come and go. The levels of procedural development, documentation, record-keeping, and training required by an ISO 9000 quality system assure that techniques and skills will carry on even when performed by different individuals.
- *Adds value.* Some 250,000 registrations in, the evidence is clear. Facilities with advanced quality cost tracking controls almost always find that their documented quality system adds value. A

major home appliance manufacturer saw its failure rate (defined as claims per year divided by sales per year) drop by 70 percent in three years. Its warranty cost per unit declined by 76 percent during the same period.

OPPORTUNITY

ISO 9000 works. Not overnight, and not without pain. It's no panacea, but it works.

Dupont, a pioneer in quality improvement and in ISO 9000 implementation, measured improvements under ISO 9000 in several different categories, including:

- On-time delivery increased from 70 percent to 90 percent.
- Cycle time improved from 15 days to one-half a day.
- First pass yield improved from 72 percent to 92 percent on a product line.
- One site reduced the number of test procedures from more than 3,000 to 2,000.

Lloyd's Register Quality Assurance, the British quality assurance registrar, published a survey of some 400 of its ISO registrants in the United Kingdom. The population was a proportional sample of market sectors and organization sizes. Some of the findings:

- 67 percent felt that the ISO 9000 approach was essential for creating and maintaining viable quality management systems.
- Most originally sought ISO for external benefits, but discovered that internal benefits were more beneficial.
- 86 percent stated that their ISO 9000 systems improved management control.
- 73 percent felt that ISO 9000 quality systems enabled them to deliver better service to customers and ensured consistency.
- 69 percent reported that ISO 9000 improved productivity and efficiency.
- 89 percent agreed that the internal benefits of ISO 9000 "met or exceeded expectations."

In a 1998 survey, a consulting firm found that "improving quality management and product quality" was cited most often as the main benefit of implementing ISO 9000. Other benefits cited included improvement in consistency, reduction in variability, and expansion of customer base.

5. What is the ISO?

> ### CAPSULE ANSWER
>
> ISO is an international standards development body, including among its membership national Standards bodies from 127 of the world's leading industrial nations.

ISO is not an acronym. It is a nickname for the International Organization for Standardization. The word "isos" is the Greek root for the word "equal" (isometric, isosceles, etc.). Which fits the organization since ISO (usually pronounced "ice-oh," not "eye ess oh") is one of the world's largest organizations involved in creating and publishing international standards to promote world trade.

Formed in 1947 and based in Geneva, Switzerland, ISO counts some 127 nations as member bodies (actively involved in the nearly 3,000 technical committees and other activities of the organization), correspondent members, and subscriber members.

ISO's stated objectives are:

■ To promote development of standardization to facilitate international exchange of goods and services.
■ To promote cooperation in intellectual, scientific, technological, and economic activity.

The chief product of ISO is a body of international agreements that are then published as voluntary international standards. The volume of this work is impressive—the ISO catalog lists some 12,000 Standards. They address nearly every field of commercial activity except electrical and electronic engineering, which are dealt with by a separate body, the International Electrotechnical Commission (IEC). Together, ISO and IEC comprise the largest nongovernmental system for voluntary industrial and technical collaboration.

Most of ISO's member groups are national standards bodies incorporated by the public laws of their respective countries. The rest—including the U.S. representative, ANSI (American National Standards Institute)—are nongovernmental organizations. Member groups are organized into several thousand technical committees, each responsible for a particular field of standards. For example, there are technical committees on welding (TC/44), essential oils (TC/54), small craft (TC/188), and sieves (TC/24). The technical committee responsible for ISO 9000 is TC/176.

The creation of an international standard begins with discussions among the members of the technical committee. These discussions result in the creation of a committee draft, which is circulated among committee members for analysis and comment. When the committee reaches consensus on the draft, it is published by ISO as a draft international standard and is submitted to all ISO member bodies for voting. Publication as an international standard requires the approval of at least 75 percent of member bodies casting votes.

ISO generally supports the development of more industry specific standards such as QS-9000. ISO 9000 has always been intended to serve as a basic quality system standard, upon which individual industries and suppliers/customers can add their own, more specific requirements.

ISO's role is limited to the development, publication, and revision of Standards. It does not enforce, regulate, or audit. Nor does it publish, or plan to publish, quality standards more specific to particular products or services.

Beyond the requirements documents (ISO 9001: 2000), ISO does provide broad-based interpretive guidance. This includes a series of documents covering:

- Application of the standards (generally).
- Application of the standards to general product/service categories, including services, processed materials, and software.
- Dependability management.
- Quality improvement.
- Quality planning.
- Configuration management.
- Auditing.
- Management of measuring equipment.

These documents are not part of ISO 9001: 2000, but they can be very helpful in the interpretation and application of the new portions of the requirements.

6. What is ISO 9000 registration or certification all about?

CAPSULE ANSWER

Registration is objective evidence that your organization meets the requirements of ISO 9000.

Registration is documented and objective evidence that an organization's quality system meets the requirements of ISO 9000.

Certification is a term often used interchangeably with registration. In the context of ISO 9000, they mean the same thing. *Registration* is the technically correct term for verification of compliance to standards of *quality systems. Certification* usually applies to verification of the quality of *products* (as opposed to quality systems).

Registration is carried out by independent companies called *registrars* (Question 7). These companies are:

■ Wholly independent.
■ Accredited by a recognized international accreditation body (Question 93).
■ Selected, and paid, by you.

Registration can cover:

■ The sole location of a single-location organization.
■ Multiple locations of a multilocation organization.
■ Only certain parts of a multilocation organization (under certain conditions).
■ Separate locations under separate certificates. (This is a more costly approach.)

The registration body audits your quality system against the requirements of ISO 9000. It reports its findings in writing. These findings may (and usually do) include noncompliances (Question 96). Major noncompliances must be closed out prior to official registration.

When this has been done, the registration body:

■ Lists the organization's name in its book of registered companies— in effect, registers the organization in its book.
■ Issues a certificate to the registered organization. This registration includes:
— Identity of the organization.
— Location(s) covered by the registration.
— A list of products/services supplied by the registered locations.
— Revision date of the Standard.
— Registration effective dates.
— Name and location of registrar.

Most registrars limit registrations to three years. After that, you must renew your registration by undergoing another complete systems audit. Some registrars do not use the renewal approach. They simply keep checking the system via surveillance audits.

PITFALL

Organizations should not select annual (rather than semi-annual) surveillance unless and until their quality management system is firmly implemented and working well.

Whichever the scheme, the organization, to keep registration, must undergo a surveillance assessment every so often. Six months is the typical interval. Some registrars offer annual surveillance schemes (not recommended except for firms with exceptionally well-implemented quality management systems). Surveillance assessments are scheduled events (there is no such thing as a "surprise" surveillance audit). Only part of the quality system is checked at each surveillance. Usually, the registrar does not disclose what part will be assessed until the day of the assessment, although some registrars will tell you everything up front. The entire quality system is usually checked via surveillance audits over the course of three years.

There is no way to "fail" a surveillance assessment, just as there is no way to "fail" a registration audit (Question 96)—except by refusing to implement corrective action required by the registrar. Normally, registrars allow adequate time, but corrective actions must be done in a timely and agreed upon manner to keep registration.

One final note: As mentioned, each registrar publishes a list of the firms it has registered to ISO 9000. A comprehensive list of ISO 9000 registered firms is available from Irwin Professional Publishing (703-591-9008).

7. What is a quality systems registrar?

CAPSULE ANSWER

A registrar audits quality systems, registers conforming quality systems to ISO 9000, and oversees continued conformance to the Standard.

A registrar, or registration body (the preferred term), is sometimes called a *certification body*. (Accreditation bodies are entirely different—they are the entities that audit/approve registration bodies.) There are some 573 registration bodies in operation worldwide, including 52 in the United States.

The registrar is the organization that checks your quality system and confirms that it meets ISO 9000 requirements for a prescribed and agreed period of time.

To do this, the registrar:

■ Audits your organization's quality system to determine the degree of conformity to ISO 9000 standards. The audit is carried out:
— On paper (desktop study).
— On site (throughout your facility).
■ Registers your quality system, assuming it conforms, to ISO 9000.
■ Monitors conformity on an ongoing basis by means of regular re-audits and other methods.

All quality system registrars perform these functions, with certain variations. Registrars differ in two principal ways:

■ Accreditation status.
■ Scope of accreditation.

Reputable ISO 9000 registrars are *accredited* by international accreditation bodies. These enforce a standard, EN 45012 (European Standard for Bodies Certificating Suppliers' Quality Systems), that governs the processes that registrars follow. This standard is quite strict:

- Registrars must make their services available to all qualified suppliers without imposing undue financial or other conditions, and must administer their regulations in a nondiscriminatory manner.
- The registrar's organization must not engage in activities that may affect its impartiality. For example:
  — It must not provide consulting services "on matters to which its certificates are related" (i.e., quality systems). This requirement is superseded by the ISO 9000 restriction noted earlier.
  — It must not directly engage in commerce with firms that it has assessed and/or registered.
  — Individuals involved in the registration process must not have provided consulting services to registration clients, or any related firms, within the previous two years.
  — Its employees and agents must not engage in business activities that would cause others to question the firm's impartiality.
  — The registrar may not market consultancy and registration services together, and may not recommend consulting services to clients.
  — Auditors may not give advice as part of registration audits.
  — The registrar must provide the accreditation body with documentation of its employees' qualifications.
  — The registrar must have appropriate facilities for carrying out its activities.
  — The registrar must have a quality manual and documented procedures. (Curiously, EN 45012 does not require that registrars register to ISO 9000!)
  — Registrars may not grant or renew certificates of registration until all major noncompliances are eliminated.

Another point of differentiation is *scope of accreditation*. All registrars are not accredited, or approved, to register firms in any line of business. Each registrar is accredited to operate within the business or industrial sectors about which it has documented expertise. This is generically referred to as the registrar's *scope*.

For information on the other ways that registrars vary and guidance on how to select the best registrar for your needs, see Question 93.

8. What is the cost of registering to ISO 9000?

<table>
<tr><td>CAPSULE ANSWER</td></tr>
<tr><td>The total cost of implementing ISO 9000 depends on factors that vary by organization and situation.</td></tr>
</table>

This was the question you turned to first, right? One fairly prominent consultant likes to answer that question this way: "Less than a million."

Kidding aside, there is only one short, definitive answer that applies to all: It depends. There are two kinds of costs to figure here:

1. The cost of implementing the system.
2. The costs to engage the registration body not only for the registration audit itself, but also for associated activities: pre-assessment, surveillance assessments (Question 94).

IMPLEMENTATION COSTS

It takes time and energy and physical resources to implement an ISO 9000 system and prepare for registration audit. This translates into money. There is no question about it. (Note, however, that it should never increase your overhead to *operate* your ISO 9000 system, once it is implemented and has reached steady state (Question 11).

How much does it cost to implement? There are so many factors to consider, it is impossible to put any kind of meaningful dollar figure here. Head count is a big factor. The more people you have, the more training you have to do. But beyond that, the best we can do is to list the factors that could cause implementation to cost "more" than average or "less":

- Your implementation will tend to cost more if:
  — You have more than one location.
  — You are design responsible.

— You have no active quality system now.
— You are undergoing any kind of significant corporate change, such as:
  ■ Downsizing.
  ■ Chapter 11 reorganization.
  ■ Merger/acquisition.
  ■ Implementing significant new process.
  ■ Implementing new EDP system.
  ■ Relocating/reconfiguring.
■ Your implementation will tend to cost less if:
— You already operate a documented quality system (Q1, Targets for Excellence, Pentastar). (But not necessarily.)
— You dedicate a seasoned, responsible manager to champion the effort. (This person would probably become the Management Representative.) Once registration is achieved, he or she would go back to prior job duties, inasmuch as the ISO 9000 responsibility would, at best, be a 25 percent job.
— You hire a good consultant to guide you.

OPPORTUNITY

Getting experienced help for implementation (even temporary or contract help, i.e., consultant) costs more in the short term, but saves much in the long term, since you'll avoid repetition, redundancy, and rework of your system.

What?? you ask. Hiring a consultant would save us money? Odds are, yes—if the consultant you hire is in fact a good one (Question 90).

It is fairly easy to estimate the costs of the following activities directly related to the implementation:

■ Overview training—30 minutes of time for every employee in the organization.
■ Orientation training—perhaps 90 minutes of time for every employee in the organization. (This is a hard one to call.)
■ Documentation writing training—Two days of time for perhaps 12 to 15 key operations people from a cross section of the organization.

- Internal audit training—Two days of time for a number of employees equal to about 10 percent of your head count.
- Internal audit costs (this one is very iffy)—An average of 4 hours per audit for 2 auditors (total of 8 hours per audit), times the number of standard operating procedures in your system (at least 20, could be as many as 26). Remember that at least one complete cycle of internal audits must be completed before registration audit.
- Equipment, supplies, and so on, including a good computer with word processing software and the services of someone who knows how to use it.

PITFALL

While you may need to add resources temporarily during implementation, avoid adding extra headcount to *operate* your quality system. If such seems needed, then your system has not been well designed.

There are other costs that are almost impossible to estimate:

- *Management representative (MR) time.* The typical MR does not work on the project full time. He or she usually has other responsibilities. Many MRs do much of their ISO 9000 work on an overtime basis, especially during implementation.
- *Document review time.* Managers and others need to review standard operating procedures and other documents, make notes, suggest changes, and so on.
- *Corrective/preventive action activities.* This is a hard one to call. If your organization already has such activities in place, then ISO 9000 will not add a lot of time to it. If your organization's activities in this regard are informal and hit-or-miss, the activity will take the time of key people, especially while they are learning how the system works.
- *Document control activities.* This burden usually falls on the MR and/or his or her staff. Once the system is set up and running, it does not seem to take up a lot of time—*as long as you keep your document system as lean as possible!* (If you let your document system bloat out to dozens and dozens of SOPs, etc., then I have no sympathy for you.)

REGISTRATION COSTS

These can vary also, but at least they are a bit easier to get your arms around. All you have to do is get quotes from a number of reputable registrars (Question 93), analyze, compare, and caveat emptor.

Registrars usually price their services on a sliding scale governed by three factors:

■ Design responsibility.
■ Number of locations (if a multisite registration).
■ Size of facility in terms of number of employees. This translates into the number of audit days required by ISO 9000 and published in a schedule (Question 7).

But then, registration costs can vary all over the place. Registrars have different daily rates. Some have application fees, and some do not. Some have annual administration fees, and some don't. Turning competing registration quotes into "apples and apples" can be an exercise in and of itself.

Here are some documented examples for the total cost of a three-year registration. In both cases, 5 accredited and approved ISO 9000 registrars submitted bids based on the same information:

■ A Tier 1 manufacturer with two manufacturing sites, a satellite warehouse, full design responsibility, and about 400 employees: $41,000 to $60,000.
■ A Tier 2 manufacturer with one site, no design responsibility, and about 100 employees: $11,500 to $24,000.

These are real numbers, but you should use them as very rough guides only. Keep in mind, also, that prices are declining. This is because ISO 9000 registration is, in large part, a market driven process, and competition on price is intense. You are free to negotiate price also, and that is strongly recommended.

But you should never let price alone be the determining factor in your selection of a registrar (Question 93).

9. How long does it take to register to ISO 9000?

CAPSULE ANSWER

Registration time depends upon the state of the quality system at inception, as well as other factors. Generally, the registration process can take between 10 and 18 months to complete.

As with the cost of registration (Question 8), the time it takes to get registered varies.* But we are talking months here, not weeks. For one thing, you have to keep running your business. You cannot simply shut down while getting registered.

The entire process can be broken down into the following general phases:

■ Implementing the ISO 9000 system.
■ Operating it for the minimum time. (A minimum of three, and preferably six, months before registration audit.)
■ Selecting a registrar. This can be done during the registration process, to save time.
■ Interval between application and registration audit. This depends on the registrar's backlog.

The time it takes to implement the ISO 9000 system depends in large part on where you are when you start. If you already have any of the following, implementation time should be relatively short:

■ A documented quality system of any kind that is active, meaningful, but not necessarily compliant with any particular standard.
■ Resources temporarily dedicated solely to implementing the system.
■ The guidance of a good consultant (with stress on the word *good*) (Question 90).

---

* This answer assumes that you want a system that is meaningful and adds value. It is possible to develop a "paperwork facade" in three months or so and then brazen and deceive your way through audits and surveillances. No reputable registrar or consultant participates in such fakery, but unfortunately for the integrity of the process, it does happen.

PITFALL

Do not attempt ISO 9000 registration if you are, at the same time, embroiled in such major initiatives as merger/acquisition, implementation of new computer system, and so on.

If you are starting from square one, implementation can take a long time. (Unless you can shut down operations while implementing—but who can do *that?*) Here are some other factors that can extend the time it takes:

■ Multiple locations.
■ Head count.
■ Whether or not you are design responsible.
■ Corporate turmoil.
■ Lack of ongoing, consistent, persistent top management commitment. This exhibits itself in a host of symptoms, including lack of sufficient resources, other issues taking priority, vacillation, failure to pay attention, failure to learn and understand, and failure to lead.

OPPORTUNITY

This is not a horse race. Take the time to do it right.

All that being said, experience has shown the following:

■ On average, the shortest interval for the entire process—from launch through registration audit—seems to be around 6 to 9 months.
■ At the other extreme, it's been known to take 18 to 24 to 36 months, even with significant resources and full management commitment.

On average, for the typical organization (whatever that is), you are looking at 10 to 18 months to get the job done.

10. What are the benefits of ISO 9000 registration?

CAPSULE ANSWER

ISO 9000 registration improves customer confidence, provides access to markets, improves competitive standing, and reduces supplier quality assurance program costs.

The benefits start when you implement (Question 4) and accrue whether you get registered or not. Registration simply leverages those benefits.

By "going for registration," you are setting a tangible goal for the entire organization to rally around. As implementation moves along, more and more employees get drawn into the effort. By the time of the registration audit, virtually everyone in the organization is aware of what's going on. (At least, they had better be!) And when the effort of many months pays off by "passing" the registration audit, it is a real morale booster for the entire organization.

But, as has been said, registration is not the checkered flag. It is the green flag. It does not signal a easing of efforts. It triggers greater efforts. And registration does not simply mean that "Great, now our customers will get off our back." It brings other benefits, too. These can include:

- *Gives customers confidence* that your firm can meet its quality commitments. Customers don't have to audit you themselves. Nor do they have to take your word for it. They have the judgment of a qualified, objective third-party registrar. And not just once. Their judgment is renewed on an ongoing basis, via surveillance audits (Question 97).
- *Provides access to markets.* Most companies registering to ISO 9000 today are doing so because key customers are pressuring them to do so. But, huge though this market is, it is just one market. There are other markets that put great store in ISO 9000 registration, as well. You would do well not to ignore them.
  — If you make and/or market products covered by EU product directives—or plan to do so in the future—you may be compelled to register your quality system in order to operate in the European Union.

— Increasingly, other marketplaces may become less and less friendly to unregistered firms as the number of registrations increases.
— In a recent survey, more than 80 percent of respondents said ISO 9000 registration would influence their choice of suppliers.
— If you are like many companies, you are finding that ISO 9000 registration is often an item on supplier surveys.

PITFALL

ISO 9000 registration can have the effect of shifting costs from customer to supplier, since many customers discontinue auditing registered suppliers. That makes it even more important that you keep your system as lean and overhead-free as possible.

■ *Reduces cost of customers' supplier programs.* To the extent that customers accept ISO 9000 registration in lieu of supplier quality assurance audits, their own costs go down.
■ *Reduces operating costs.* British Standards Institution (BSI), possibly the world's largest and most respected quality assurance registration body, estimates that registered firms reduce operating costs by 10 percent on average. However, don't take this number to the bank; a great deal of how much the system contributes depends on your starting point. If you are already operating at peak efficiency, ISO 9000 registration is not going to pay back at that rate.
■ *Provides competitive advantage.* ISO 9000 registration is a powerful marketing tool for its holder. Registered firms proudly display their certificate and logo, and their names appear in registries of approved firms. Quality is already a strong differentiator in parity markets. ISO 9000 registration is objective, confirmed evidence of an active, thriving quality system.
■ *Reduces supplier quality assurance (SQA) audits.* Some companies are subject to as many as 30 to 40 supplier quality audits a *month!* As ISO 9000 gains visibility and credibility, the fact of registration is increasingly easing acceptance to approved supplier lists. In some cases, it eliminates supplier audits entirely.

11. How can we keep our ISO 9000 system from fading away?

CAPSULE ANSWER

Your ISO 9000 system will not fade away as long as management sees value in maintaining the system.

The dreaded "program-of-the-month" syndrome: Here today, with much sound and fury—and, after a slow, embarrassing fade-away— gone tomorrow.

Your ISO 9000 system won't fade away as long as top management remains committed to it. Top management will remain committed to it as long as they see that it is returning some sort of benefit. That benefit may take one of two general forms:

1. Current business stays as a result of the ISO 9000 system.
2. New business comes as a result of the ISO 9000 system.

PITFALL

Improvement programs fade away when tangible benefits are not recognized by management.

Net result: Organization achieves incremental cost savings as a result of the ISO 9000 system. Since most companies get into ISO 9000 due to customer pressure, the first benefit is the most operative one. The second benefit is speculative. The net result, surprisingly, is genuine— ISO 9000 registrants, with virtually no exception, realize proven cost savings—but, like mating elephants, it is accompanied by much roaring and screaming, and takes two years to see the results.

THE REINFORCEMENT MECHANISMS

1. Surveillance assessments.
2. Management reviews.
3. Internal audits.
4. Measurement and analysis.

Top management will stay committed to the system if only to maintain existing business and, hopefully, obtain new business. This requires that the organization remain registered. For the organization to remain registered, it must undergo and pass surveillance assessments, usually every six months. This is probably the most potent of the four reinforcement mechanisms of ISO 9000—the attributes that keep the system from fading away as another program of the month.

The second reinforcement mechanism is the Management Review process required by the Standard (Question 31). Management reviews require that senior management review the ISO 9000 system from top to bottom—its implementation, its suitability, its effectiveness, its results. Management must do this on a scheduled basis. Records must be kept to prove that it is done. The reviews have the effect of forcing management to pay attention to the system. The reviews are also an educational process for management. Over time, they see how useful the ISO 9000 system can be as a management and communications tool.

The third reinforcement mechanism is the internal audit process required by the Standard (Questions 68, 85, 86). Trained, independent employees audit the entire quality system on a scheduled basis and record the results. Corrective actions must be carried out and verified against deficiencies found during these audits. Internal auditing is not only an outstanding implementation tool. It also keeps the entire organization tuned in to the system and improving it on an ongoing basis.

OPPORTUNITY

The disciplined gathering and analysis of objective data about your process is the surest route to meaningful improvement.

The fourth reinforcement mechanism—and arguably the most important one—is the measurement and analysis processes required by the Standard (Questions 63–67). If you do a good job of establishing meaningful process and quality measures—and then gather, analyze, and react to the data on a disciplined basis—you will see how well the system is working for you. Word to the wise: *Establish the measures early in the implementation,* so you have a set of baseline measures to compare with subsequent results.

12. We're leaders in our market. Our customers love us. Our quality is unquestioned. What does ISO 9000 offer us that we don't have already?

Capsule Answer

ISO 9000 can help your company maintain access to key customers, improve performance, and achieve a new level of international credibility.

What does ISO 9000 offer? For one thing, it offers you continued business with customers who may be requiring you to register. That is a pretty strong benefit right there.

These customers may never question your quality, but these customers depend heavily on their main suppliers. They know they can improve their quality and through-put, if you improve yours.

- *Just because you are great does not mean you are as great as you could be.* ISO 9000 mandates a continuous improvement system. You can wriggle and fudge, but if you implement that system and work it conscientiously, you cannot help but improve. Continuous improvement is not just a buzz term. It is an imperative.
- *Just because you are great today does not mean you will be great tomorrow.* Has your industry changed? Has your organization changed? A well-implemented ISO 9000 helps your organization adapt to change. It brings independence of individuals and consistency of practices—two features that tend to resist declines in performance.

Opportunity

ISO 9000 implementation and registration are tangible and meaningful messages to customers that you are committed to their satisfaction.

What else does ISO 9000 bring you? When well implemented, an ISO 9000 quality system improves organization performance. That is, after all, the whole point. In cases where it does not, the fault tends not to be in the ISO 9000 process (its inherent deficiencies notwithstanding). When an ISO 9000 system does not provide substantial benefits and improvement in performance (Question 4), it is usually because management has consciously chosen to cut corners, blow smoke, stay uninvolved, and starve the system of all but the most essential resources. "We'll do this stupid thing, but we're sure not going to change the way we operate."

ISO 9000 registration brings you one more thing that your organization may not have today: International credibility. ISO 9000 is deployed and practiced in nearly 100 countries around the world. In today's ever-growing international economic climate, this is not a bad emblem to have, however narrow the scope of your market today.

PART TWO

Technical Requirements and Guidelines

This section describes the *requirements* of ISO 9000: 2000. These are the rules you must follow, the processes you must implement. They're presented more or less in the order in which the Standard is written, except that certain elements of common interest (i.e., process development, management, improvement) are grouped together for convenience.

This section also summarizes the associated *Guidelines for Performance Improvement* written in ISO 9004: 2000. For convenience, it is grouped with the requirements.

Do not assume that the order of presentation is the order in which the processes should be implemented. A suggested implementation order is discussed in Question 76.

Included with each question is:

- A brief narrative about the requirement.
- Indication as to whether written procedures are *required* or *recommended* (Question 18).
- Indication as to whether records are required.
- A summary of the specific requirements.
- A summary of the related guidelines (from ISO 9004: 2000).
- Pitfalls and opportunities.
- A capsule answer.

Those upgrading from ISO 900X: 1994 will want to consult the section that explains whether the requirement is new. If it is not, a brief narrative explains the differences, if any, between the ISO 900X:

1994 and ISO 9001: 2000 clauses. Upgraders should also consult the questions and answers in the last section: ISO 9001: 2000—Making the Transition.

One final note: This text is based on ISO/DIS 9001: 2000 and ISO/DIS 9004: 2000, released by ISO in December, 1999. The "final" approved version, scheduled for November 2000, may vary to some extent.

Great care has been taken to paraphrase the requirements, to render them in layperson terms, and to melt out redundancies, excessive wordiness, illogical order, legalese, and so on. Great care has also been taken to retain the essence of the content. That said, you are cautioned that you will, should you go forward with registration, be audited *NOT* to the language of this book, but to the text of the ISO 9001: 2000 Standard as formally approved and implemented. So the text here is no replacement for reading and understanding the ISO 9001: 2000 Standard itself.

Rules of the Road

13. What is the overall requirement for the quality management system?

CAPSULE ANSWER

You must devise, implement, maintain, and improve a quality management system that meets the requirements of the Standard.

The prerequisite here is that you have defined your processes (Question 39). Now the Standard requires you to establish a quality management system (QMS) that meets the requirements of the Standard—for the purpose of *applying* those processes and *demonstrating* them.

PITFALL

Lack of adequate implementation is a frequent noncompliance raised during registration audits.

Those concepts are related, yet different. The QMS *demonstrates* the processes by communicating their workings to various audiences: employees, customers, auditors, regulatory bodies (where applicable), even suppliers in certain instances. The QMS, being at its core a set of written documents, is what you say you do. And there must be no variation between what it says and what you *actually* do.

This means the QMS must be applied—another word for *implemented*. This concept is very important. The quality management system must not be a solitary, stand-alone, pro-forma exercise—a pack of paper in a three-ring notebook up on a shelf somewhere. The QMS must be at the very heart of what your organization does. An *implemented* QMS is a blueprint by which your processes convert inputs into outputs to meet customer needs. Not just today, but tomorrow; therefore the QMS must be *maintained*. And, recognizing the inexorable forces of change (in the needs of customers, the strength and smarts of competitors, etc.), the QMS must also be *improved* by the organization.

PITFALL

Maintaining a QMS requires the same discipline as maintaining a swimming pool. It's not hard work to keep up, but you have to do what's required, and walk the talk, every day. Let things slide and you have disaster on your hands.

ISO 9001: 2000 Requirements		
Title Quality management system—General requirements		
Clause 1.1	**SOP*** None	**Records Required?**** No
Summary of Requirements		
The Standard lists generic quality management system (QMS) requirements where any size or type of organization providing any type of product needs to: • Prove it can consistently provide product that meets customer and applicable regulatory requirements, and • Satisfy customers by effectively applying the system, improving it, and preventing nonconformity.		
*Question 18. **Question 22.		

ISO 9004: 2000 Guidelines—Performance Improvement
Title   Quality management systems—Requirements
Clause 1.1 Scope—General
Summary of Guidelines
The effort to provide satisfaction should extend beyond customers to all other interested parties (owners, suppliers, society, etc.) To monitor customer satisfaction, the organization should evaluate information relating to customer perceptions as to the organization's success at meeting customer requirements.

Transition Guidance: ISO 9001: 1994 to ISO 9001: 2000	
ISO 9001: 1994 Cross-Reference	1.0 Scope
Summary of Differences	Essentially the same. The need for the system to address regulatory requirements (besides customer requirements) is new. So is the statement about continual improvement, and the explicit statement that the Standard is generic and applicable to all.
Quality Policy Manual Updates	4.2: Insert language addressing regulatory requirements (as relevant) and continual improvement.
Procedure Updates	Where needed, develop/edit procedures to address regulatory requirements. (Continual improvement is covered elsewhere.)
See Question	99, 100

14. Do all the requirements of the Standard apply to us?

CAPSULE ANSWER

You may be exempt from certain requirements of the Standard due to the unique nature of your customer needs and your products, services, and processes.

Not necessarily. It depends on the needs of your customers, and the nature of your organization and its processes. The Standard allows you to "tailor" your QMS to take these things into account, in effect rendering certain requirements of the Standard "not applicable."

PITFALL

Typically, *design* as understood in the Standard means black box design—designing products/services virtually from scratch. Modifying existing designs does not necessarily obligate you to meet the control of design and development requirements. This gray area is best sorted out by a reputable and experienced consultant and/or your registration body.

For example, if your organization is like 80 percent of them, it produces its product and service from *established designs.* In other words, you do not create the designs. They exist already, and/or are provided to you by customers or others. If this is the case, then the requirements for design and development (Questions 43–49) do not apply. (*But* if you have design capability and *ever* use it on behalf of customers, then the requirements *do* apply.)

The same holds true for any of the requirements in Section 7 of the Standard (Product Realization). Certain processes referenced in that section may not apply to you, due to the unique nature of your customers' needs, the products/services you provide, and the processes you use to provide them. If this is the case, then you can reduce the scope of your QMS and label the related requirements as not applicable.

There are several important provisos, including:

- "Permissible exclusions" applies only to the requirements listed in Section 7 of the Standard. All other requirements of the Standard apply to everyone.
- "Permissible exclusions" does not relieve you of the obligation to meet customer needs and requirements.
- "Permissible exclusions" does not exempt you from meeting applicable regulatory requirements. And you may not use regulatory requirements to claim exemption from meeting requirements of ISO 9001: 2000.

If you are eligible for reduced scope and tailoring of the requirements, you explain same in your quality policy manual (Question 20).

ISO 9001: 2000 Requirements		
Title Permissible exclusions		
Clause 1.2	**SOP*** None	**Records Required?**** No
Summary of Requirements		
The organization may exclude quality management system (QMS) requirements due to: • The nature of the organization's product. • Customer requirements. • Applicable regulatory requirements. The organization may exclude only QMS requirements that: • Do not affect its ability to meet customer and applicable regulatory requirements. • Appear in clause 7. The organization may not claim conformity to the Standard if it exceeds permissible exclusions. This includes exclusions that may be permitted via fulfillment of regulatory requirements .		
*Question 18. **Question 22.		

Transition Guidance: ISO 9001: 1994 to ISO 9001: 2000	
ISO 9001: 1994 Cross-Reference	4.2 Quality system
Summary of Differences	This requirement is new.
Quality Policy Manual Updates	Add language addressing requirement to quality manual. Indicate in quality manual which requirements (from Section 7 of the Standard) have been excluded, with justification.
Procedure Updates	None needed.
See Question	99

15. How does ISO 9001 relate to ISO 9004?

CAPSULE ANSWER

ISO 9001 is the requirements document to which you are audited; ISO 9004 is a guidance document for improved performance to which you are not audited.

ISO 9001 and ISO 9004 are both standards. But ISO 9001 is the *minimal* set of quality standards considered necessary to assure that customer satisfaction is consistently met. ISO 9001 is the starting point. It's what you are audited to.

ISO 9004 is a parallel document with (mostly) the same numbering scheme and subject headings. It is an *expansion* of ISO 9001. Its guidelines are meant to help organizations improve their overall performance beyond what they achieve by meeting the minimal requirements of ISO 9001. You are not audited to ISO 9004 (but you can certainly audit yourself to it via your internal audit process [Question 68] if you choose to).

This element of the Standard also acknowledges the existence of other documented management systems pertaining to environmental protection, health/safety, and finance. ISO 9001 and ISO 9004 only tangentially addresses such matters. Again, you are free to incorporate such issues into your ISO 9001 system if you want to—and it is a highly recommended way to leverage your investment in ISO 9001.

Guidance (from ISO 9001 and ISO 9004: 2000)	
Title	Relationship between ISO 9001 and ISO 9004, and with other management systems
Clause	0.3, 0.4
Summary of Guidance	
ISO 9001: 2000 and ISO 9004: 2000 are a consistent pair of quality management system (QMS) standards. Structured in parallel, they can be used separately or together. • ISO 9001: 2000 specifies minimum QMS requirements needed for achieve customer satisfaction by meeting specified product/service requirements. It is for internal use, or for certification or contractual purposes. • ISO 9004: 2000 addresses an expanded set of QMS objectives aimed at helping organizations improve performance. It is not intended for certification or contractual purposes. ISO 9001: 2000 does not address environmental, occupational, health/safety, or other requirements, but may be integrated with them.	

16. How does ISO 9001 relate to other management systems such as environmental or safety management?

CAPSULE ANSWER

ISO 9001 does not include environmental, safety, or other management systems, but may be integrated with them where practical.

ISO 9001: 2000 acknowledges the existence of other documented management systems pertaining to environmental protection, health/safety, and finance. ISO 9001 and ISO 9004 only tangentially address such matters. You are free to incorporate such issues into your ISO 9001 system if you want to.

If your organization is subject to regulations/standards for environmental protection, health/safety, and so on, it is an excellent idea to fold these systems into your ISO 9001 system so that your people become accustomed to a single *business system*.

Guidance (from ISO 9001 and ISO 9004: 2000)	
Title	Relationship between ISO 9001 and other management systems
Clause 0.4	
Summary of Guidance	
ISO 9001: 2000 does not address environmental, occupational, health/safety, or other requirements, but may be integrated with them.	

17. What is the overall nature and structure of the quality management system?

CAPSULE ANSWER

You must define and document the QMS, implement it, and continually improve it.

This is a sort of umbrella requirement for the quality management system (QMS). It specifies what management is supposed to do to, first, *develop* the QMS. These steps are to *document* it, per the requirements of the Standard (Question 18) and *implement* it (Questions 74–88).

The requirement breaks out what is meant by the word *implement*. You're required to define and identify the processes, sequence them, and define how they interact. You must further ensure that the processes are effective by defining:

■ *Methods* (best practices—approved ways of doing things).
■ *Criteria* (objectives against which the results of the processes are measured).
■ *Information* that is needed to operate the processes effectively.

Finally, in a major departure from ISO 9001: 1994, the Standard requires that the system be *continually improved*. This requires monitoring, measurement, analysis, and ongoing action. Details for these processes are outlined in Questions 63–73.

The strong sense of this requirement is that the QMS is not expected to be a stand-alone project, at a distance from the organization's processes for meeting customer needs. Rather, the QMS is expected to be at the heart of these processes.

ISO 9001: 2000 Requirements		
Title Quality management system requirements		
Clause 4.1	**SOP*** None	**Records Required?**** No
Summary of Requirements		
As required by the International Standard, the organization must establish a quality management system (QMS). It must be: • Documented. • Implemented. • Maintained. • Managed. • Continually improved. To implement the QMS, organization must: • Define QMS processes. • Determine process sequence and interaction. • Ensure effective process operation and control by defining criteria and methods. • Ensure the availability of information needed to operate and monitor processes. • Measure, monitor, and analyze processes. • Implement action needed to achieve planned results and continually improve.		
*Question 18. **Question 22.		

ISO 9004: 2000 Guidelines—Performance Improvement	
Title	Managing systems and processes Use of quality management principles
Clause	4.1 4.3
Summary of Guidelines	

To enable the organization's systems and processes to be clearly understood, managed, and improved, the organization should:
- Define its systems and processes.
- Ensure effective process operation and control.
- Ensure effective control of measures and data used to determine satisfactory performance.
- Describe and define activities and processes that can lead to performance improvement.
- Closely monitor the movement toward performance improvement.

Principles on which the International Standard rest include:
- Continual improvement.
- Customer focus.
- Factual approach to decision making.
- Involvement of people.
- Leadership.
- Mutually beneficial supplier relationships.
- Process approach.
- System approach to management.

Transition Guidance: ISO 9001: 1994 to ISO 9001: 2000	
ISO 9001: 1994 Cross-Reference	4.2.1 Quality system—general
Summary of Differences	New are requirements to *implement, manage,* and *continually improve* QMS. New also are the specified steps of implementation.
Quality Policy Manual Updates	Indicate accomplishment of the implementation phases and point to procedures where they exist. Point also to (new) procedure(s) on monitoring, analysis, and improvement.
Procedure Updates	This does not require its own procedure. But new procedures are recommended in several areas mentioned in this requirement—analysis of data (question 70) and continual improvement (question 71), which were not required by ISO 9001: 1994.
See Question	100

Documenting and Communicating the Quality Management System

18. What sorts of quality documentation must we have?

CAPSULE ANSWER

You must implement procedures and instructions to describe and control the processes required to assure that product/service meets customer needs.

First, you design your processes (Question 39). Then you develop a quality management system (QMS) that covers the requirements of the Standard and helps you to implement the defined processes (Question 13 and 17). Now we come to the heart of the matter. You must document the QMS as specified in the Standard.

Some clauses of the Standard require written procedures. Most do not. But the Standard does include criteria for when procedures and other documents should be implemented. It's a basic judgment call requiring you to take into account:

- Your organization's size.
- The complexity of the process(es).
- The skill of your people.

If you have excluded certain requirements from the scope of your QMS (Question 14), obviously you need not have procedures for these elements.

The table on page 39 lists the requirements of the Standard section by section. For each, it indicates whether a procedure is *required* or *recommended*. The recommendations (which you should consider as guidelines only) are based on:

- The author's field experience with organizations of many kinds.
- Awareness of the areas where quality system assessors usually expect to see written procedures.

No.	Title	Procedure	Question
1.0	Quality system requirements—Scope— General	None	13
1.2	Permissible exclusions	None	14
4.2	Documentation requirements	None	18
5.1	Management commitment	None	23
5.2	Customer focus	None	24
5.3	Quality policy	Recommended	26
5.4.1	Quality objectives	Recommended	27
5.4.2	Quality planning	Recommended	28
5.5.2	Responsibility and authority	None	29
5.5.3	QMS—Management representative	None	30
5.5.4	QMS—Internal communication	Recommended	19
5.5.5	QMS—Quality manual	None	20
5.5.6	QMS—Control of documents	Required	21
5.5.7	QMS—Control of records	Required	22
5.6	Management review	Recommended	31
6.1	Provision of resources	None	32
6.2	Human resources	Recommended	33–34
6.3	Facilities	Recommended	36
6.4	Work environment	Recommended	38
7.1	Planning of realization processes (Quality planning)	Required	50
7.2.1	Identification of customer requirements	Recommended	52
7.2.2	Review of customer requirements	Recommended	53
7.2.3	Customer communication	Recommended	51
7.3	Design and development	Recommended	43–49
7.4	Purchasing	Recommended	54–56
7.5.1	Operations control (production and service operations)	Recommended	57
7.5.2	Identification and traceability	Recommended	59
7.5.3	Customer property	Recommended	60
7.5.4	Preservation of product	Recommended	61
7.5.5	Validation of processes	Recommended	40
7.6	Control of measuring and monitoring devices	Recommended	62
8.1	Measurement, analysis, and improvement—Planning	Recommended	64
8.2.1	Customer satisfaction—measurement and monitoring	Recommended	65
8.2.2	Internal audit	Required	68
8.2.3	Measurement and monitoring of processes	Recommended	41
8.2.4	Measurement and monitoring of product and/or service	Recommended	58
8.3	Control of nonconformity	Required	69
8.4	Analysis of data	Recommended	70
8.5.1	Planning for continual improvement	Recommended	71
8.5.2	Corrective action	Required	72
8.5.3	Preventive action	Required	73

Note that it is *not* necessary to write a separate procedure for each of these. You are free to construct your system in whatever manner is best suited for your particular situation.

Procedures are often called Level 2 documents. Procedures define processes, and typically have a moderate amount of detail. The quality policy manual (Question 20), which is Level 1, defines policies, and is the least detailed of all.

PITFALL

More often than not, when it comes to procedures, organizations err on the side of "quantity" vs. quality. "More" is definitely not better. "More" does not impress auditors or make it more likely that you will "pass" (whatever that means). All "more" is expensive. Be selective. Err on the side of leanness. Strive for the smallest possible set of the shortest possible documents. And avoid squint print.

Level 3 documents are required by the Standard, also, where appropriate. These are called instructions, or more familiarly work instructions. They are used to define the best practices for carrying out *tasks,* and tend to be the most detailed of all. Work instructions usually spell out the approved methods for the following types of tasks:

- Inspection.
- Calibration,
- Production (where activities and sequence must be precise, or quality could be adversely affected).
- Production tasks where quality of work cannot be independently judged.
- Data processing tasks that are complex and intricate.

The Standard includes language that offers a great deal of flexibility in the range, detail, and scope of the procedures and instructions. Clearly, you do not have to spell out in infinite detail every single blessed thing that is ever done within every minute task of the process. *But,* you must define the processes themselves in procedures; you must specify "best practices" in procedures and instructions where the lack of same could cause undesirable variation or a direct or indirect failure to meet customer needs fully. This only makes good business sense.

OPPORTUNITY

Here's your chance to find out what the best process practices really are. And it won't cost you a cent. The expertise is right under your roof, in the brains of the people in the trenches who make their living helping your organization meet customer needs. They are the process owners, the subject matter experts; if you develop the procedures with them in the lead, you'll be amazed at the results.

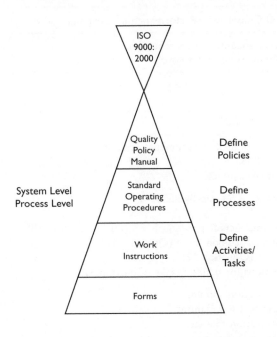

ISO 9001: 2000 Requirements		
Title Documentation requirements		
Clause 4.2	**SOP*** None	**Records Required?**** No
Summary of Requirements		

The organization must prepare, in any form or type of media:
- Documented procedures required by the Standard,
- Documents needed to ensure effective operation and process control.

The extent of system documentation must be consistent with:
- Competence of personnel doing the work.
- Organization size and type.
- Process complexity and interaction.

*Question 18.
**Question 22.

ISO 9004: 2000 Guidelines—Performance Improvement
Title   General documentation requirements   Documentation and records
Clause 4.2   5.5.5
Summary of Guidelines

The main purpose of quality documentation is to:
- Describe the QMS.
- Express the quality policy.

Quality documentation typically includes:
- Forms.
- Policy documents including the quality manual (Question 20).
- Process control documentation (Question 57).
- Quality records (Question 22).
- Work instructions for defined tasks (Question 57).

Process documentation should:
- Be appropriate to the organization.
- Support organization's needs.
- Be in any form or in any media suitable to organization's needs.
- Include methods for system implementation, maintenance, and improvement.

Requirements for documentation and records may arise from:
- Contractual requirements.
- Decisions by the organization.
- Industry sector standards.
- Statutory and regulatory requirements.

Transition Guidance: ISO 9001: 1994 to ISO 9001: 2000	
ISO 9001: 1994 Cross-Reference	4.2.2 Quality system procedures
Summary of Differences	Mostly new, with a bit of old thrown in, and generally less prescriptive. ISO 9001: 1994 required the implementation of many more procedures; ISO 9001: 2000 leaves many issues open to judgment calls. ISO 9001: 2000 defines "implementation" only in a note, which is guidance only, and does not mention work instructions. ISO 9001: 2000 also provides for documents to exist in any form or media.
Quality Policy Manual Updates	Update quality manual with language from this section.
Procedure Updates	None needed (already covered by other procedures)
See Question	99

19. What sorts of communication activities are we required to implement?

CAPSULE ANSWER

You are required to establish processes for communicating the status of the QMS throughout the organization.

You are required to define processes for communicating the status and effectiveness of the QMS among the various levels and functions of the organization. You are expected, in other words, to make the QMS and its status (successes, opportunities, etc.) visible on an ongoing basis.

This requirement, which is new to ISO 9001: 2000, is yet another aspect of the revised Standard aimed at placing the QMS squarely at the center of the operations of the organization. Ongoing communications about the QMS will prevent it from being, or becoming, a marginalized after-thought.

OPPORTUNITY

Leverage your existing communications channels (newsletters, etc.) to include the types of information specified in this requirement.

Effective communication serves another critical quality purpose. Very often, business problems (including quality problems) are, ultimately, communications problems.

ISO 9001: 2000 Requirements		
Title Internal communication		
Clause 5.5.4	**SOP*** Recommended	**Records Required?**** No
Summary of Requirements		
Among its levels/functions, organization must ensure communication regarding: • Processes of the QMS. • Process effectiveness.		
*Question 18. **Question 22.		

ISO 9004: 2000 Guidelines—Performance Improvement
Title   Communication
Clause 5.5.4
Summary of Guidelines
As resources for improvement and the involvement of people in achieving quality objectives, define and implement processes to communicate quality: • Accomplishments. • Objectives. • Requirements. Potential venues include: • Audio-visual/electronic media. • In-house publications. • Meetings. • Notice boards. • Team briefings.

Transition Guidance: ISO 9001: 1994 to ISO 9001: 2000	
ISO 9001: 1994 Cross-Reference	4.2 Quality system
Summary of Differences	This requirement is new.
Quality Policy Manual Updates	Add language addressing requirement to quality manual.
Procedure Updates	Recommend development of process and implementation of procedure defining the process.
See Question	99

20. What kind of quality manual must we have?

CAPSULE ANSWER

You are required to create and maintain a quality manual that describes the QMS and cross-references to procedures and other QMS documents.

The quality manual is the "top level" document in the QMS. As such, it ties directly to the requirements of the Standard and describes how the organization's QMS meets the requirements of the Standard. The quality manual also specifies the elements of the Standard that are not addressed by the QMS because of the unique characteristics of the organization. In other words, if the organization is not design responsible, then the design requirements need not be addressed by the QMS; the quality manual describes such "permissible exclusions" (Question 14).

The most important thing about the quality manual is that it is a *policy document only*. In most organizations, it does not spell out how processes are carried out. This is done in the so-called "level 2" documents (Standard Operating Procedures) (Question 18). Therefore, the typical quality manual is fairly generic. Once completed, it tends not to change much except when the organization undergoes radical change.

OPPORTUNITY

Though the typical quality manual closely mimics the requirements of the Standard to make the system easier to audit, "auditability" should not be the primary objective of the manual. Readability, clarity, and understanding should be.

The quality manual is almost always the first document seen by the registration body during the registration process (Question 94). It is therefore very important that the manual look good, read well, and meet all the requirements of the Standard. Since the quality manual may be used for marketing purposes (i.e., to show prospective customers), it must include no organization confidential information.

The typical quality manual includes the following:

- Quality policy statement (Question 26).
- Statement of management commitment.
- Organization chart(s) (Question 29).
- Outline of QMS document structure (Question 18).
- Cross-reference to elements of ISO 9001: 2000.

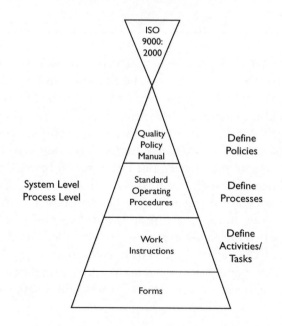

Remember that you are free to structure your document system any way you want to, as long as the requirements of the Standard are met. Smaller organizations may choose to combine the quality manual and system level procedures into one document or book. Generally speaking, though, it is more practical to keep them separate. Procedures change much more frequently than the quality manual does and tend to require wider circulation. Procedures will sometimes include sensitive process information, so they should not be combined with the quality manual (which may be circulated outside the organization).

Most organizations start with some sort of quality manual template. This is not a bad idea—as long as the "final" quality manual accurately reflects the specific characteristics of the organization and its policies, especially with respect to quality.

ISO 9001: 2000 Requirements		
Title Quality manual		
Clause 5.5.5	**SOP*** None	**Records Required?**** No
Summary of Requirements		
The organization must establish, maintain, and control a quality manual that includes: • Description of the sequence and interaction of QMS processes. • Details/justification for exclusions (see Question 14). • Documented procedures or reference to them. • QMS scope.		
*Question 18. **Question 22.		

ISO 9004: 2000 Guidelines—Performance Improvement
Title   Quality manual
Clause 5.5.5
Summary of Guidelines
See Question 18.

Transition Guidance: ISO 9001: 1994 to ISO 9001: 2000	
ISO 9001: 1994 Cross-Reference	4.2.1 Quality system—general
Summary of Differences	New is reference to outlining "permissible exclusions," plus the description of process sequence and inter-action. New also is mention that manual must be con-trolled (although this was implicit before in element 4.5).
Quality Policy Manual Updates	Add section on permissible exclusions. If it does not already exist, outline sequence and interaction of processes (could be in graphical form).
Procedure Updates	None needed.
See Question	14

21. How must we control the documents in our quality system?

CAPSULE ANSWER

You must ensure that only the latest approved versions of quality related documents (external as well as internal) are reasonably available to employees that need them.

Essentially, you are required to assure that employees have ongoing reasonable access to the current and approved versions of quality system documents that impact their jobs.

PITFALL

Document control is not a value-added activity. Minimize the cost by keeping the population and length of documents at a minimum.

What documents are we talking about? First of all, this refers to the *internally generated* documents that are specific to the quality system, including:

- Procedures (Question 18).
- Work instructions (Question 57).
- Quality policy manual (Question 20).
- Forms.

It also applies to internally generated documents that are referenced by the Standard and used within the quality system. These include documents such as:

- Drawings/blueprints.
- Approved vendor lists (Question 54).

The procedure you are required to write must spell out how these documents are approved, circulated, updated/reapproved, and withdrawn when obsolete. You must have some method for readily identifying the *current revision level* of quality system documents (such as a master list). If you maintain obsolete documents for historical purposes, these must be clearly identified as obsolete. Ultimately, only the "latest and greatest" (and legible, please!) versions of quality system documents must be in use.

PITFALL

Document control is often THE largest source of audit noncompliances. When implementing, seek out "informal" instructions, forms, and so on, and be sure to include them in your document control system.

The requirement also talks about *documents of external origin* that impact the quality system and/or your customers. Examples of these include:

- Customer specifications.
- Drawings.
- Standards (such as ISO 9001: 2000, ANSI Standards, etc.).

The Standard requires that such external documents be "identified and controlled." Therefore, revision control, circulation control, removal of obsolete versions, and so on, are as important with externally generated documents as they are with internally generated ones. Keep this in mind as you develop your system.

OPPORTUNITY

Technology savvy organizations automate some or all of their quality system document circulation by putting it online via PC networks, intranets, and so on. This can seriously reduce the expense of administering document control. Just make sure that *all* people affected by the documents have *reasonable* access to them.

ISO 9001: 2000 Requirements		
Title Control of documents		
Clause 5.5.6	**SOP*** Required	**Records Required?**** No
Summary of Requirements		
Documents required for the quality management system must be controlled. A documented procedure must be established to: • Approve documents for adequacy before issue. • Ensure that documents remain legible, readily identifiable, and retrievable. • Ensure that relevant versions of needed documents are available where used. • Ensure that documents of external origin are identified and their distribution controlled. • Identify current revision status of documents. • Prevent the unintended use of obsolete documents, and to apply suitable identification to them if they are retained for any purpose. • Review documents, update them as needed, and re-approve them.		
*Question 18. **Question 22.		

ISO 9004: 2000 Guidelines—Performance Improvement
Title   Documentation and records
Clause 5.5.5
Summary of Guidelines
To ensure that correct documents are used, control of documentation should be: • Defined. • Implemented. Remove from issue points, or otherwise prevent from unintended use, all obsolete documents.

Transition Guidance: ISO 9001: 1994 to ISO 9001: 2000	
ISO 9001: 1994 Cross-Reference	4.5 Document and data control
Summary of Differences	Reworded, but no substantive changes.
Quality Policy Manual Updates	None.
Procedure Updates	None needed.
See Question	101

22. What records are we required to keep?

CAPSULE ANSWER

You are required to maintain certain records to show that your QMS meets requirements and operates effectively.

The Standard requires that you keep records sufficient to show that you are meeting the requirements of the Standard, and that the QMS is operating effectively. In the procedure you are required to implement, you must spell out how the records are identified, stored, retrieved, and protected. You must define retention times for all records, and spell out what happens to records when that retention time has passed.

OPPORTUNITY
Use the ISO 9001 implementation process as an opportunity to organize your records and "de-junk" your facility.

Records are the best evidence of ongoing conformity, which makes them important during internal (Question 68) and external audits (Question 95). Records are also resources for various corrective (Question 72) and preventive actions (Question 73) and problem-solving activities.

PITFALL
Many assessors require that quality records be kept in ink (not pencil). Many also prohibit the use of "white-out" to make corrections to quality records.

The following table lists two types of records. The first are the records that must be kept by *all* organizations. The second type of records may or may not have to be kept by your organization, depending on whether or not the requirements are relevant to you. If the requirements are not relevant, then you will have exercised the "permissible exclusions" clause of the Standard (Question 14) and need not keep the associated records.

Clause	Title	Must Be Kept By		Question
		All Organizations	Organizations for Which Requirement Is Not Excluded	
5.6.3	Management review output	x		31
6.2.2	Training, awareness and competency	x		34
7.1	Planning of realization processes		x	50
7.2.2	Review of product requirements		x	53
7.3.2	Design and/or development inputs		x	44
7.3.3	Design and/or development outputs		x	45
7.3.4	Design and or development review		x	46
7.3.5	Design and or development verification		x	47
7.3.6	Design and/or development validation		x	48
7.3.7	Design and/or development changes		x	49
7.4.1	Purchasing control		x	54
7.5.2	Identification and traceability		x	59
7.5.3	Customer property		x	60
7.6	Control of measuring and monitoring devices		x	62
8.2.2	Internal audit	x		68
8.2.4	Measurement and monitoring of product	x		58
8.3	Control of nonconformity	x		69
8.5.2	Corrective action	x		72
8.5.3	Preventive action	x		73

ISO 9001: 2000 Requirements		
Title Control of quality records		
Clause 5.5.7	**SOP*** Required	**Records Required?**** No
Summary of Requirements		

Records required for the QMS must be maintained to provide evidence of:
• Conformance to requirements.
• Effective QMS operation.

A written control procedure must be established for ensure quality record:
• Disposition.
• Identification.
• Protection.
• Retention time.
• Retrieval.
• Storage.

*Question 18.
**Question 22.

ISO 9004: 2000 Guidelines—Performance Improvement
Title   Documentation and records
Clause 5.5.5
Summary of Guidelines

Documents to be kept, and quality performance records, should be:
• Controlled.
• Maintained.
• Protected.

The organization should maintain records sufficient to:
• Demonstrate conformance to requirements.
• Verify effective QMS operation.

Records are a resource of knowledge for QMS maintenance and improvement. Analyze them to provide:
• Ideas for process improvements.
• Information for use in the QMS improvement.
• Inputs for corrective and preventive action.

Transition Guidance: ISO 9001: 1994 to ISO 9001: 2000	
ISO 9001: 1994 Cross-Reference	4.16 Control of quality records
Summary of Differences	Essentially the same. Shorter and more generic.
Quality Policy Manual Updates	None needed.
Procedure Updates	None needed.
See Question	—

Management's Responsibilities for Quality

23. What are the overall requirements for top management?

CAPSULE ANSWER

Management must demonstrate its commitment to establishing the quality management system.

The Standard is very specific about the role of top management in the implementation of the QMS. This element, new in ISO 9001: 2000, serves as a kind of "umbrella" to other requirements later in Section 5.

PITFALL

When ISO 9000 implementations struggle, the cause is almost universally traceable to lack of 100 percent management commitment. Lip service will not do. Only walking the talk will do.

The overall requirement is that management "provide evidence of its commitment to the establishment of the quality system." As has been learned through long and hard experience, organization change (such as implementation of a quality system) cannot be a bottom-up process. It has to be top-down. Management has to lead. The effectiveness of the QMS is directly proportional to the willingness and ability of top management to lead. Consistently, persistently, without alibis or excuses.

Beyond that, this requirement specifies activities for top management that are referenced elsewhere. Management must perform management reviews (Question 31), implement a quality policy and objectives (Questions 26 and 27), emphasize the importance of meeting customer legal and regulatory requirements (Questions 25, 51, 52), and provide resources (Questions 32–38).

In all this, ISO 9001: 2000 puts a bright spotlight on the responsibilities of *top* management (as differentiated from management in general) that was not so evident in the earlier Standard.

ISO 9001: 2000 Requirements		
Title Management commitment		
Clause 5.1	**SOP*** None	**Records Required?**** No
Summary of Requirements		
Top management must prove its commitment to developing/improving the quality management system (QMS) by: • Communicating to the organization the importance of meeting customer, regulatory, legal requirements. • Conducting management reviews. • Establishing quality policy/objectives. • Providing needed resources. To achieve customer satisfaction, top management must ensure that customer needs and expectations are: • Determined. • Converted into requirements. • Fulfilled.		
*Question 18. **Question 22.		

ISO 9004: 2000 Guidelines—Performance Improvement
Title   Management responsibility—general guidance
Clause 5.1
Summary of Guidelines

The key to achieving benefits for interested parties is to sustain and increase customer satisfaction. To develop and maintain an effective and efficient QMS that achieves benefits for customers and all other interested parties, essential are top management:
• Commitment.
• Involvement.
• Leadership.

Top management responsibilities include:
• Achieving continual improvement.
• Identifying realization processes that add value for the organization.
• Leading the organization.
• Maintaining current performance.
• Managing change.
• Planning for the organization's future.
• Providing resources.
• Providing organization structure.
• Setting and promoting policies and objectives to increase awareness, motivation and involvement of people.
• Setting and communicating directions related to achieving satisfaction of interested parties.

Top management should establish and implement, consistent with the organization's purpose:
• Plans.
• Policies.
• Strategic objectives.

Management should involve everyone in the organization in these actions.

Top management should identify the organization's realization processes directly related to the organization's success. Top management should also identify those support processes that affect:
• Needs of interested parties.
• Process efficiency.

To ensure all processes operate as an efficient network, the organization should analyze process interaction. Examine and monitor:
• Definition and control of inputs, activities and outputs.
• Process sequence and interaction, to ensure they achieve desired results.
• Risks and opportunities.

(continued)

(Continued)

To manage each process, define a process owner with full authority and re-sponsibility for achieving process objectives.

To verify achievement of strategic objectives, top management should define a process that measures the organization's performance. This process could include:
- Assessment of satisfaction of customers (Question 65) and other inter-ested parties (Question 67).
- Financial measures.
- Process performance measures (Question 41).

To ensure maintenance and development of the QMS as the organization structure changes, top management should consider as options, when deter-mining the best option for organizational improvement, radical change as well as continual (incremental) improvement.

To ensure that continual improvement drives organizational development, input performance information to management review (Question 31).

Transition Guidance: ISO 9001: 1994 to ISO 9001: 2000	
ISO 9001: 1994 Cross-Reference	4.1 Management responsibility
Summary of Differences	This requirement is new.
Quality Policy Manual Updates	Add language addressing requirement to quality manual.
Procedure Updates	None needed.
See Question	99

24. What are top management's obligations with respect to the customer?

Capsule Answer

Top management must achieve customer confidence by understanding their needs/expectations, and aiming the organization's processes at meeting them.

Overall, top management is required to aim the organization and its process squarely at earning the confidence of customers. This means developing clear understanding of customer needs/expectations, and then organizing processes and subprocesses in such a way that the needs and expectations are consistently met.

Understanding customer needs requires a relentless thirst for information. First, top management needs to obtain and maintain a thorough understanding of customers themselves: categories, classifications, and detailed facts about needs, preferences, and expectations. Understanding customer needs requires knowledge not just about customers themselves, but also about the environment surrounding them. This means doing research on competition, as well as benchmarking.

Then top management must translate all that knowledge into action by implementing processes aimed at achieving customer needs (as defined in the requirements of Sections 6 and 7).

The success of the organization ultimately depends on meeting customer needs. Top management is ultimately responsible for organizational success. It follows, then, that top management must make the fulfillment of customer needs a primary part of its activities, and a top priority. Because, after all, without customers, nothing else matters.

The guidelines extend this concept beyond customers to make recommendations for ways of meeting the needs of other stakeholders, including people (employees), owners, suppliers, and society.

ISO 9001: 2000 Requirements		
Title Customer focus		
Clause 5.2	**SOP*** None	**Records Required?**** No
Summary of Requirements		
With the aim of achieving customer satisfaction, top management must ensure that customer needs and expectations are: • Determined. • Converted into requirements. • Fulfilled.		
*Question 18. **Question 22.		

ISO 9004: 2000 Guidelines—Performance Improvement

Title   Needs and expectations of interested parties

Clause 5.2

Summary of Guidelines

Every organization has interested parties, each with needs and expectations. Categories include:
• Customers and end users.
• Owners/investors.
• People in the organization.
• Society.
• Suppliers and partners.

Organizational success depends on understanding and satisfying current and future needs and expectations of customers (including end-users), and other interested parties. Management should endeavor to exceed the expectations of all interested parties. To do so:
• Identify the needs and expectations of all interested parties.
• Maintain balanced response to interested parties' needs and expectations.
• Translate needs and expectations into requirements.
• Communicate requirements to all organization levels.
• Improve processes to create value for the interested parties.

Customer and end-user product concerns include:
• Availability.
• Conformance.
• Delivery.
• Dependability.
• Life-cycle costs.
• Post-realization activities.
• Price.

To define customer and end-user needs and expectations:
• Determine key product characteristics for the customers and end-users.
• Identify and assess market competition.
• Identify opportunities, weaknesses and future competitive advantages.
• Identify customers, including potential customers.

To ensure the strongest possible involvement and motivation of people, identify their needs and expectations for:
• Competencies.
• Development of knowledge.
• Recognition.
• Work satisfaction.

Define financial and other results which satisfy the identified needs and expectations of owners and investors.

(Continued)

Define financial and other results which satisfy the identified needs and expectations of owners and investors.

Consider the potential benefits of establishing partnerships with organization's suppliers that create value for both parties. Base partnerships on the definition of joint strategies and sharing of knowledge, risks and profits. When establishing partnerships:
- Identify key suppliers, contractors and distributors as potential partners.
- Jointly establish a clear understanding of customers' needs and expectations.
- Jointly establish a clear understanding of the partners' needs and expectations.
- Set goals to secure opportunities for continuing partnerships.

In considering its relationships with society:
- Consider environmental impact, including conservation of energy and natural resources.
- Demonstrate responsibility for health and safety.
- Identify the current and potential impacts of products, processes, and activities on society in general, and the local community in particular.
- Identify applicable statutory and regulatory requirements.
- Define the needs and actions for improvement in all areas.

Transition Guidance: ISO 9001: 1994 to ISO 9001: 2000	
ISO 9001: 1994 Cross-Reference	4.1 Management responsibility
Summary of Differences	This requirement is new.
Quality Policy Manual Updates	Add language addressing requirement to quality manual.
Procedure Updates	None needed.
See Question	99

25. Do the quality system requirements make any reference to legal rules/regulations?

CAPSULE ANSWER

You should have a procedure defining a process for identifying legal requirements that affect quality aspects of your product/service.

No. But the ISO 9004 guidelines for performance improvement do call this out. To the extent that legal requirements affect "quality aspects" of your products/services, you should have a process for identifying those requirements and addressing them.

OPPORTUNITY

Consider uniting your quality, environmental, and safety systems into one overall "business system," following the ISO 9001: 2000 model.

This requirement affects some organizations much more than others. It is also one of those *self-evident* notions. If, for example, your process is affected by environmental regulations, you no doubt already have implemented systems for meeting them. You've had no choice. This guideline is important because, through it, your quality system is linked to whatever processes you have for dealing with legal rules and regulations.

Doing this keeps your ISO 9001: 2000 system from becoming just a stand-alone subprocess, off to the side from your safety, environmental, financial, and other subprocesses. Instead, your quality system becomes part of an integrated "whole"—a documented system for operating your business.

ISO 9004: 2000 Guidelines—Performance Improvement
Title   Statutory and regulatory requirements
Clause 5.2.3
Summary of Guidelines
Ensure that organization has knowledge of the statutory/regulatory requirements applicable to: • Activities. • Processes. • Products. Consider also: • Benefits to interested parties from exceeding compliance. • Organization's role in protecting community interests. • Promoting ethical interpretation of and effective compliance with current and prospective requirements. Responding to relevant statutory and regulatory requirements should not stop the organization from meeting quality objectives.

26. What sort of "quality policy" is management expected to set?

CAPSULE ANSWER

Top management is required to document its quality policy—including commitment to customer needs and continual improvement—and make it known throughout the organization.

The top management of your organization must establish its "quality policy" and make it known throughout the organization. What is a "quality policy"? It is a written expression of top management's definition of quality, beliefs about quality, commitment to quality. It is the central theme, the rallying cry, around which the organization operates. It is a very small set of principles about quality to which top management commits itself, consistent with which top management requires employees to operate, and from which top management dares not deviate.

As you might expect, the Standard does not get very specific about the elements to include in the quality policy. It has to include a commitment to meeting requirements—requirements of the Standard, and, most especially, requirements of the *customer*. It has to be appropriate to the needs of customers and the organization. It must link to quality objectives (Question 27). And it must include a commitment to continual improvement.

OPPORTUNITY

This is your chance to send a message directly to customers about not only your commitment to meeting their needs, but also your commitment to improvement.

This is, then, much more than simply a generic white-bread one-size-fits-all mission or vision statement layered with cliches and warm fuzzies. Just as the beliefs and purposes of organizations and their customers are quite specific, so must the quality statement be specific. Just as organizations and their customers are unique, so must the quality policy statements be unique. Just as organizations and their customers evolve, grow, and change, so must the quality policy statements evolve and change (per the periodic suitability reviews the Standard requires).

The quality policy statement ought to come straight from the pen of the top management group, the object of painstaking thought and effort. It ought to be no more than 50 words in length. It ought to be clearly distinguishable, in content, language, and tone, from those of other organizations, especially organizations in the same markets or fields. And it should include a capsule or "slogan" version, to be taught through repetition and promotion to the entire workforce.

Finally, the quality policy must be *controlled* (Question 21) so that its issues can be retrieved when and as the policy changes.

ISO 9001: 2000 Requirements		
Title Quality policy		
Clause 5.3	**SOP*** Recommended	**Records Required?**** No
Summary of Requirements		
Top management must ensure that the quality policy: • Includes a commitment to meeting requirements and to continual improvement. • Is appropriate to organization's purpose. • Is communicated and understood at appropriate organization levels. • Is controlled (Question 21). • Is reviewed for continuing suitability. • Provides a framework for establishing and reviewing quality objectives.		
*Question 18. **Question 22.		

ISO 9004: 2000 Guidelines—Performance Improvement
Title Quality policy
Clause 5.3
Summary of Guidelines
In establishing the quality policy, top management should consider: • Contributions of suppliers and partners. • Expected level of customer satisfaction. • Needs of other interested parties. • Opportunities and needs for continual improvement. • Resources needed. An effectively formulated and communicated quality policy should: • Address continual improvement and customer satisfaction. • Be periodically reviewed and revised as necessary. • Be consistent with organization's overall business policies and vision of the future. • Demonstrate top management commitment to quality and provision of adequate resources for its achievement. • Make quality objectives understood throughout the organization. • Promote, with management leadership, quality commitment at all levels of the organization.

Transition Guidance: ISO 9001: 1994 to ISO 9001: 2000	
ISO 9001: 1994 Cross-Reference	4.1.1 Management responsibility—quality policy
Summary of Differences	Stronger and more specific. New is requirement that quality policy must include commitment to meeting requirements and continual improvement. New also is requirement that policy be reviewed on an ongoing basis.
Quality Policy Manual Updates	Add language to this effect.
Procedure Updates	Recommend creating procedure covering how quality policy is created, reviewed, communicated.
See Question	100

27. What sorts of quality objectives are we required to set?

Capsule Answer

You are required to set objectives for quality of products/services, consistent with quality policy and the principle of continual improvement.

Under the Planning section, the organization is required to set quality objectives. These must be set "at each relevant function and level." So it is not enough simply to specify *how* quality processes and tasks must be done. You must also set *goals/objectives* for the outcomes of quality processes and tasks. They must also be tied to requirements for products/services, in other words, to meeting customer needs.

Opportunity

Include employees in the effort to set process-based objectives. You'll be pleasantly surprised at the height of the hurdles they will often set for themselves.

The Standard is careful to keep us from setting our sights too low. It requires us to set objectives consistent with "commitment to continual improvement." So objectives should be challenging. They should be an incentive always to do better and to achieve more.

Objectives should be specific and measurable (Question 63). The reference to "function and level" notwithstanding, objectives should be process-based. Establish objectives at the overall process level first, specific to customer and organization needs. Then define subobjectives at subprocess, function, and, as relevant, task levels. That said, be careful to keep your set of objectives lean and meaningful. And, though the Standard does not require it here, review objectives for suitability and effectiveness from time to time.

ISO 9001: 2000 Requirements		
Title Planning—quality objectives		
Clause 5.4.1	**SOP*** Recommended	**Records Required?*** No
Summary of Requirements		
Top management must ensure that quality objectives: • Are consistent with the quality policy. • Are established at relevant organization functions/levels. • Are measurable. • Include commitment to continual improvement. • Include objectives for meeting product requirements.		
*Question 18. **Question 22.		

ISO 9004: 2000 Guidelines—Performance Improvement
Title Planning—quality objectives
Clause 5.4.1
Summary of Guidelines
Establish quality objectives during the planning process, taking into account: • Current and future needs of the organization. • Markets served. • Output from management reviews. • Performance of current products and processes. • Satisfaction levels of all interested parties. Objectives should be: • Capable of being measured. • Clearly communicated to all relevant people. • Consistent with the quality policy. • Deployed throughout the organization with defined responsibility for their achievement. • Periodically reviewed. • Revised as necessary. • Translatable by people into objectives for their individual contributions.

Transition Guidance: ISO 9001: 1994 to ISO 9001: 2000	
ISO 9001: 1994 Cross-Reference	4.2.3 Quality system—quality planning
Summary of Differences	This requirement is new.
Quality Policy Manual Updates	Add language addressing requirement to quality manual.
Procedure Updates	Recommend development of process and implementation of procedure defining the process.
See Question	99

28. How are we required to plan our quality system?

CAPSULE ANSWER

You are required to maintain a process for planning the processes required to meet customer need—and for changing those plans as required.

The Standard requires planning literally from top to bottom. At the top are the quality objectives (Question 27); quality planning must address how you will meet these. This means planning out the processes you will employ to meet customer needs and expectations— by producing and/or delivering products and services. Within the processes, you should plan how you will *verify* that the "quality characteristics" of the products/services meet customer needs.

Planning must also address the requirements of the Standard, including any *permissible exclusions* from the requirements that you will deploy (Question 14).

An important part of the planning requirement involves *organizational change*. Your planning process must ensure that change is "controlled" (a tall order!) and that the QMS is maintained during change. This requirement, new in ISO 9001: 2000, is obviously the result of practical experience. In organizations for whom the QMS is a mere paperwork exercise, it can often "go on hold" during times of drastic change. This requirement is intended to keep that from happening.

In a sense, the planning requirement is an "umbrella requirement" that is exploded into more specific requirements in later sections (especially Section 7—Product Realization). But the Standard clearly intends for planning to be a separate and distinct process, with separate and distinct deliverables.

ISO 9001: 2000 Requirements		
Title Quality planning		
Clause 5.4.2	**SOP*** Recommended	**Records Required?**** No
Summary of Requirements		
Top management must identify and plan the resources needed to achieve quality objectives. Planning output must be documented. Quality planning must address: • Continual improvement of QMS. • Needed resources. • QMS processes, considering permissible exclusions (Question 14). Planning shall ensure that: • Change is controlled. • QMS integrity is maintained during changes.		
*Question 18. **Question 22.		

ISO 9004: 2000 Guidelines—Performance Improvement
Title   Quality planning
Clause 5.4.2
Summary of Guidelines

Quality planning is integral to the QMS. Implement quality planning for the activities and resources needed to satisfy:
- Quality objectives.
- Quality policy.
- Requirements.

Primary inputs for quality planning include:
- Lessons learned.
- Needs/expectations of customers and other interested parties.
- Opportunities for improvement.
- Performance of QMS processes.
- Product performance.
- Risk assessment and mitigation.

Outputs of quality planning can identify:
- Alternative planning needs.
- Improvement approaches, methodology and tools.
- Indicators for performance achievement.
- The need for documentation and records.
- The resources needed.
- The responsibility and authority for execution of improvement plans.
- The skills and knowledge needed.

As the organization changes, review/revise quality planning outputs.

Transition Guidance: ISO 9001: 1994 to ISO 9001: 2000	
ISO 9001: 1994 Cross-Reference	4.2.3 Quality system—quality planning
Summary of Differences	More generic; less prescriptive. New is requirement that quality planning address continual improvement of QMS. New also is requirement for change control.
Quality Policy Manual Updates	Add language to quality manual covering new issues.
Procedure Updates	If procedure covering quality planning does not now exist, one is strongly recommended to address how quality plans (which must be documented) are developed, used, maintained, updated, and so on.
See Question	100

29. How are we to define responsibility and authority?

CAPSULE ANSWER

You must define the responsibility, authority, and interrelationship of all functions that affect quality, and communicate this information effectively to all who need it.

To work effectively, and meet quality requirements, people within the organization need to know:

- What their roles and functions are.
- What they are responsible to do.
- How they relate to each other.
- The range and extent of their authority and freedom to act.

The Standard requires that you define all this and communicate it clearly and effectively to people in the organization. This is without question management's most critical communications job. Management can't expect people to know what to do unless and until they are clearly and consistently told. So it's best to do this in writing. The question is: In what form?

Many organizations, especially larger and more traditional ones, default to job descriptions. And this can be an effective way to go, within the limits described here. If your organization already uses job descriptions—and the job descriptions are complete and current, you can adopt these as part of your quality system as part of meeting this requirement. The problem with job descriptions tends to be twofold:

1. Often they are not up to date.
2. Very often they are extremely long, wordy, and unwieldy.

PITFALL

Organization charts should depict *job functions,* not the names of individuals. This keeps them from having to be revised so frequently.

If your organization does not use job descriptions now (or the job descriptions that exist are outdated and/or incomplete), embarking on a job description crusade is not the most effective way to meet this requirement. There are much simpler, cleaner ways. First of all, you can easily define responsibility and authority in the procedures and instructions (Question 18) that you have to write for the QMS anyway. As to interrelationship of functions, you can easily and effectively communicate that via one or more organization charts.

OPPORTUNITY

Very often, addressing this requirement is the first time an organization officially defines what its employees have the "authority" to do.

As with every other document in the QMS, the documents you use to define responsibility, authority, and interrelationship must be *living* documents. As your organization changes and evolves, so must the QMS documents.

ISO 9001: 2000 Requirements		
Title Responsibility and authority		
Clause 5.5.2	**SOP*** None	**Records Required?**** No
Summary of Requirements		
To facilitate effective quality management, functions, their responsibilities and authorities, and their organizational interrelations, must be defined and communicated.		
*Question 18. **Question 22.		

ISO 9004: 2000 Guidelines—Performance Improvement
Title Responsibility and authority
Clause 5.5.2
Summary of Guidelines
To implement and maintain the QMS effectively and efficiently, top management should define and communicate responsibility and authority that: • Enables people to help the organization achieve quality objectives. • Helps establish involvement and commitment of people throughout the organization.

Transition Guidance: ISO 9001: 1994 to ISO 9001: 2000	
ISO 9001: 1994 Cross-Reference	4.1.2.1 Organization—responsibility and authority
Summary of Differences	Serious meltdown and is much more generic, but net effect is neutral.
Quality Policy Manual Updates	None needed.
Procedure Updates	None needed.
See Question	101

30. Who is ultimately responsible for running the QMS?

Capsule Answer

The management representative is responsible to top management for effectively implementing the QMS.

The Standard requires you to appoint one or more members of management to act as management representative (MR). This person (or team) is charged with ensuring that the QMS is effectively implemented and maintained.

The MR reports to top management on the status of the QMS and presents improvement opportunities as they arise. Finally, the MR is responsible for ensuring that awareness of customer requirements is maintained throughout the organization.

Opportunity

Though the MR has significant responsibilities, he or she should delegate as much as possible. People in divisions and remote sites should be assigned to act as assistant MRs for those activities.

In real life, the MR's duties (which are virtually never a full-time job) include:

- Running the document control (Question 21) system.
- Running the corrective/preventive action process (Questions 72, 73).
- Overseeing management review (Question 31).
- Interfacing with the registration body (Questions 93–96).

PITFALL

Never, ever select a newcomer to the organization to be management representative.

What are the qualifications to be MR? Keep in mind that this person, or team, is the QMS "champion." The MR must absolutely be a "believer." Beyond that, qualifications include:

- Significant knowledge of organization process(es).
- High level of seniority in the organization.
- Strong organizational and multitasking skills.
- Ability to, as needed, lead, guide, cajole.
- Direct access to highest levels of organization management.
- High degree of respect within the organization.

ISO 9001: 2000 Requirements		
Title Management representative		
Clause 5.5.3	**SOP*** None	**Records Required?*** No
Summary of Requirements		
Top management must appoint member(s) of the management who, irrespective of other duties, must have responsibility and authority including: • Ensuring QMS processes are established and maintained. • Promoting awareness of customer requirements throughout the organization. • Reporting to top management on QMS performance including improvement needs.		
*Question 18. **Question 22.		

ISO 9004: 2000 Guidelines—Performance Improvement
Title   Management representative
Clause 5.5.3
Summary of Guidelines
The goal of appointing management representative(s) is to enhance effective and efficient QMS operation. Top management should give management representative(s) authority to: • Coordinate. • Evaluate. • Manage. • Monitor QMS processes. The representative(s) should: • Communicate with customers and other interested parties on QMS matters. • Report to top management.

Transition Guidance: ISO 9001: 1994 to ISO 9001: 2000	
ISO 9001: 1994 Cross-Reference	4.1.2.3 Management representative
Summary of Differences	New is allowance for there to be more than one management representative. New also is responsibility to promote awareness of customer requirements.
Quality Policy Manual Updates	Add language covering promoting awareness of customer requirements.
Procedure Updates	Separate procedure is not needed. But MR's activities in promoting awareness of customer requirements should be included in procedures covering identification of customer requirements (Question 52), review of customer requirements (53), customer communication (51), as appropriate.
See Question	100

31. What is "management review" all about?

CAPSULE ANSWER

Top management is required to review the QMS regularly to assure its continued effectiveness.

At defined intervals, top management is required to review the status of the QMS to make sure the QMS continues to be adequate, effective, and suitable. You should implement a procedure that defines how your management review process works.

TIP

How often is often enough? During implementation, monthly is good. Afterward, 3 to 4 times per year is usually adequate.

Issues to be considered during the review include audit results, feedback from customers, assessment of process performance, and status of corrective and preventive actions. You are also expected to follow up on action items from previous management reviews, and to examine the effect of *changing circumstances* on your QMS.

OPPORTUNITY

If your organization holds regular top management strategy meetings, you could easily combine this with the management review process.

The Standard requires specific "outputs" from management review—outputs in the form of *action*. These actions may relate to audits of product, process, and/or service, or need for resources. Action should result in QMS improvement. You must also record the results of management reviews.

Management review helps keep top management (in particular) focused on the QMS. For firms that lack a collaborative management culture, management review can come as a bit of culture shock. However, organizations that pursue the process with vigor usually find it to be not just a worthwhile process, but an essential one as well.

ISO 9001: 2000 Requirements		
Title Management review		
Clause 5.6	**SOP*** Recommended	**Records Required?*** Yes
Summary of Requirements		
To ensure continuing QMS suitability, adequacy and effectiveness, top management must review the QMS at planned intervals. The review must evaluate the need for changes to: • Quality objectives. • Quality policy. • The QMS. Inputs to management review must include current performance and improvement opportunities related to: • Audit results. • Changes that could affect the QMS. • Customer feedback. • Follow-up actions from earlier management reviews. • Process performance and product conformance. • Status of preventive and corrective actions. Management review outputs must include actions related to: • Improvement of product related to customer requirements. • Improvement of the QMS and its processes. • Resource needs. Results of management reviews must be recorded.		
*Question 18. **Question 22.		

ISO 9004: 2000 Guidelines—Performance Improvement
Title   Management review
Clause 5.6
Summary of Guidelines

Top management should establish a process to review the QMS at periodic intervals. To ensure quality objectives and requirements are integral to the organization's overall objectives and requirements, make management review part of the organization's strategic planning cycle.

Management review should:
- Analyze current activities that may require change.
- Consider opportunities to improve the QMS.
- Evaluate QMS effectiveness and efficiency.
- Verify satisfaction of quality policy and objectives.

Review inputs should include:
- Analysis of product conformance.
- Changes in original assumptions.
- Financial effects of quality related activities.
- Impact of changes to relevant statutory and regulatory requirements.
- Market place evaluation, including the performance of competitors.
- Measurements of customer satisfaction and satisfaction of needs and interests of other interested parties.
- Opportunities for improvement.
- Performance of suppliers.
- Process performance.
- Results from internal, customer, third party audits of the QMS.
- Results of benchmarking activities.
- Results of organization self-assessment.
- Status and results of improvement activities.
- Status of action items from previous reviews.
- Status of corrective and preventive actions.
- Status of partnership initiatives.

Results of management review should focus on:
- Ability to introduce new product on time in the market.
- Adding value for interested parties.
- Compliance with relevant statutory and regulatory requirements.
- Improved performance of products and processes.
- Managing risks.
- Planning for future resources.
- Suitability of organizational structure and resources.

(Continued)

To facilitate monitoring of progress, and as input to subsequent reviews, record management review:
• Conclusions.
• Decisions for actions.
• Observations.
• Recommendations.

The management review process should be:
• Evaluated for effectiveness.
• Improved when necessary.

Transition Guidance: ISO 9001: 1994 to ISO 9001: 2000	
ISO 9001: 1994 Cross-Reference	4.1.3 Management review
Summary of Differences	Much more specific as to what is required in inputs and outputs and to assure that management review outcomes are acted upon.
Quality Policy Manual Updates	Update language adding new requirements.
Procedure Updates	Update to add specifics called for in new requirements. If procedure does not now exist for management review, one is strongly recommended.
See Question	100

Human and Other Resources

32. What does the Standard say about resources to operate the quality system?

CAPSULE ANSWER

You are required to identify resources needed for the QMS, and provide them in a timely way.

The Standard requires you to identify the resources needed to satisfy customers and run the QMS—and to provide them in a timely manner. It seems self-evident and intuitively obvious, but sometimes quality systems run in semi-starvation mode because management chooses not to deploy sufficient resources. It is very uncommon to see non-compliances written on this requirement, which serves as an umbrella requirement for more specific ones (Questions 33–38).

In a larger sense, this requirement is an effort to push organization management toward a strategic outlook and longer term planning of the business. As such, it fits nicely with other more strategic requirements of the Standard—such as quality policy (Question 26), quality objectives (Question 27), process management, and so on.

ISO 9001: 2000 Requirements		
Title Resource management—general requirements		
Clause 6.1	**SOP*** None	**Records Required?*** No
Summary of Requirements		
The organization must determine and provide, in a timely manner, the resources needed to: • Address customer satisfaction. • Implement and improve QMS processes.		
*Question 18. **Question 22.		

ISO 9004: 2000 Guidelines—Performance Improvement
Title   Provision of resources
Clause 6.1
Summary of Guidelines
Identify and make available resources essential to implementing strategies and achieving objectives for the QMS. These may include: • Financial resources. • Information. • Infrastructure. • People. • Suppliers. • Work environment. Consider: • Efficient and timely provision of resources in relation to opportunities and constraints. • Enhancement of competence via training. • Impact of resources on the environment. • Information management. • Intangible resources such as intellectual property. • Organization structures, including project and matrix management needs. • Planning for future resources. • Resources and mechanisms to encourage innovative continual improvement. • Tangible resources such as realization and support facilities. • Use of natural resources.

Transition Guidance: ISO 9001: 1994 to ISO 9001: 2000	
ISO 9001: 1994 Cross-Reference	4.1.2.2 Resources
Summary of Differences	Added is requirement that resources be provided in timely manner, as well as resources needed to address customer satisfaction.
Quality Policy Manual Updates	Update language to include new requirements.
Procedure Updates	Recommend developing procedure outlining process for identifying and providing resources as required.
See Question	100

33. What kind of education and skills does the Standard require our employees to have?

<table>
<tr><td>CAPSULE ANSWER</td></tr>
<tr><td>You are required to assign to jobs affecting quality people with demonstrated competence in terms of education, skills, training, and so on.</td></tr>
</table>

ISO 9001: 2000 does not require any specific education, skills, or training. But it requires you make sure that people with responsibility for quality are *competent*. This is a higher level requirement than simply proving that people have had training (although education/training are very much required also [Question 34]). People can have training without acquiring any competence at all.

<table>
<tr><td>OPPORTUNITY</td></tr>
<tr><td>When implementing, you need not reconstruct training history/records of *existing* employees. You do need to certify present employees as possessing the experience, skills, qualifications, and so on, specified for their job functions. Once the ISO 9000 system gets underway, start tracking training plans and records.</td></tr>
</table>

This means that you must, when assigning people to quality-affecting jobs, ensure that they have the competence to perform those jobs well. Competence may be inferred from experience (no doubt positive experience), as well as skills, training, and education. Objective evidence of competence may be developed by having employees undergo a "test period" on the job with closer than usual scrutiny on the outcome of their work.

The ISO 9004: 2000 guidelines for performance improvement (see below) go much further than the requirement does. They recommend methods for developing employee careers, management by objective, and recognition/reward systems.

ISO 9001: 2000 Requirements		
Title Assignment of personnel		
Clause 6.2.1	**SOP*** Recommended	**Records Required?**** No
Summary of Requirements		
Personnel who are assigned responsibilities defined in the QMS must be competent on the basis of applicable: • Education. • Experience. • Skills. • Training.		
*Question 18. **Question 22.		

ISO 9004: 2000 Guidelines—Performance Improvement
Title   Involvement of people
Clause 6.2.1
Summary of Guidelines
To achieve objectives and to stimulate innovation, encourage the involvement of people through: • Creating conditions to encourage innovation. • Defining responsibilities and authorities. • Employee selection, ongoing training, and career planning. • Encouraging recognition and reward. • Ensuring effective teamwork. • Establishing individual and team objectives. • Facilitating open, two-way communication by continually reviewing the needs of its people. • Fostering involvement in objective setting and decision making. • Identifying competence needs for each process activity. • Investigating the reasons why people are leaving the organization. • Managing performance and evaluating results. • Using information technology to facilitate communication of suggestions and opinions. • Using measurements of people satisfaction for improvement. To ensure organization's objectives are achieved, consider subcontracting or temporary employment of people.

Transition Guidance: ISO 9001: 1994 to ISO 9001: 2000	
ISO 9001: 1994 Cross-Reference	4.18 Training
Summary of Differences	Added is requirement that assigned employees be competent and skilled.
Quality Policy Manual Updates	Add language addressing the additions.
Procedure Updates	Add assessment of competence and skill to training system and associated procedure, if not there already.
See Question	100

34. What are the components of the training system required by the Standard?

CAPSULE ANSWER

Your system must assess employee competence, provide training, and assess training effectiveness. The system must assure that employees are aware of their role and impact on the quality processes.

You are required to implement procedures that, first of all, keep you abreast of the competence levels of employees in quality-affecting positions. Quite logically, your system must also provide training that fills competence gaps. To close the loop, you must have a process for checking the effectiveness of training provided. And you are required to maintain appropriate records.

PITFALL

Very often organizations do nothing to assess the effectiveness of training, thereby missing chances to leverage their training dollars.

This requirement, considerably toughened from the version in ISO 9001: 1994 (see below), makes additional important stipulations. Your training process must assure that people in quality affecting positions understand:

- The relevance and importance of their activities.
- The impact of their activities on achievement of quality objectives.

OPPORTUNITY

"On the job training" is most definitely included in the training system required by the Standard. So too is training provided to temps and contract labor.

This is another way of making employees aware that *the work they do affects quality*. It is another way of reinforcing to all employees the importance of achieving quality objectives. It integrates what have often been, unfortunately, disconnected elements within the organization: (1) objectives; (2) procedures, (3) training, (4) performance/outcomes.

People need to understand that departure from procedures and failure to meet quality objectives can adversely affect customers, sales, profits, and so on. It is very important that the quality system not become a framework or justification for implementing a "who do we fire?" approach to quality problems. Quality problems are almost always system problems, *not* people problems.

ISO 9001: 2000 Requirements		
Title Training, awareness, and competency		
Clause 6.2.2	**SOP*** Recommended	**Records Required?**** Yes
Summary of Requirements		
For people performing activities that affect quality, the organization must: • Identify competency needs. • Provide training to satisfy those needs. • Evaluate the effectiveness of the training provided. • Maintain appropriate records of education, experience, training and qualifications (Question 22). The organization must also ensure that people are aware of: • Relevance and importance of their activities. • Impact their activities have on achievement of quality objectives.		
*Question 18. **Question 22.		

ISO 9004: 2000 Guidelines—Performance Improvement
Title Competence and training
Clause 6.2.2
Summary of Guidelines

The organization should:
• Assess the competence of its people to perform the activities.
• Develop plans to close any gaps.
• Identify the competence needed for each activity that affects performance.

When identifying competence, analyze present/expected organization needs with competence of current people. Input to consider includes:
• Evaluation of the competence of individual people to perform defined activities.
• Future demands related to strategic and operational plans and objectives.
• Legislation, regulation, standards, and directives affecting the organization, its activities, and its resources.

To provide people with knowledge which, together with skills and experience, leads to competence:
• Analyze the development needs of all people.
• Consider providing personal development training.
• Design training plans for them to achieve its objectives.

Training programs should address:
• Consequences to the organization and its people of failing to meet the requirements.
• Creativity and innovation.
• Documentation for performing the work.
• Importance of meeting requirements and the needs of customers and other interested parties.
• Internal and appropriate external standards.
• Introductory programs for new people.
• Knowledge of markets and customer needs and expectations.
• Management skills and tools.
• Organization's impact on society.
• Organizational change and development.
• Periodic refresher programs for people already trained.
• Relevant statutory and regulatory requirements.
• Social skills.
• Technical knowledge and skills.
• The initiation and implementation of improvement activities.
• The organization's policies and objectives.
• The vision for the future of the organization.

(Continued)

Training plans should include:
- Evaluation of training in terms of enhanced competence of people.
- Identification of necessary resources and support.
- Measurement of the effectiveness of training and the impact on the organization.
- Training objectives.
- Training programs and methodologies.

Transition Guidance: ISO 9001: 1994 to ISO 9001: 2000	
ISO 9001: 1994 Cross-Reference	4.18 Training
Summary of Differences	Much stronger and more specific. New are requirements that training address identified competency needs (Question 33), as well as evaluation of training effectiveness. Training must now include awareness training in employee impact on quality objectives.
Quality Policy Manual Updates	Add language addressing added requirements.
Procedure Updates	Update system and related procedure to add new requirements.
See Question	100

35. Is information management mentioned anywhere in the Standard?

CAPSULE ANSWER

It is recommended that you manage your process for gathering and protecting internal and external information needed to control quality.

Information is the ultimate "resource" in today's fast-paced business environment. The *Guidelines for Performance Improvement* (ISO 9004: 2000) recognize this by devoting a section specifically to information. While not a requirement, these guidelines are well worth considering.

It is recommended that you define a process for identifying information needed to control your processes, and ensure product/service conformity. You may wish to implement a procedure covering this.

Information in these areas can arise from external as well as internal sources. Requirements for the gathering of such information appear in many places in the Standard, especially in Section 8 (Questions 63–65). Examples include information on suppliers, conformity of product/service, and process control information, among others. You may also obtain vital information via benchmarking and other external opportunities.

Such information quite often is obtained at great cost, and could easily be of high value to competitors. So protecting its confidentiality is vital. As with so many other elements in the Standard, the ISO 9004: 2000 guidance recommends that you periodically evaluate your information management system for improvement opportunities.

ISO 9004: 2000 Guidelines—Performance Improvement
Title   Information
Clause 6.5
Summary of Guidelines
Information is: • A fundamental resource for the continual development of an organization's knowledge base. • A source of innovation. • Essential for making factual decisions. To manage information effectively, the organization should: • Ensure appropriate security and confidentiality. • Identify internal and external sources of information. • Identify its information needs. • Provide timely access to adequate information. • Use information to meet its strategies and objectives. Evaluate information management for effectiveness and efficiency. Implement any potential improvements.

36. How is infrastructure addressed by the Standard?

CAPSULE ANSWER

You are required to provide and maintain the infrastructure elements (plant, equipment, services) needed to assure that product/service meets customer and internal requirements.

Quite simply, the Standard requires you to provide the types of infrastructure elements needed to assure that your quality/service meets customer and internal requirements. General areas include your facilities, equipment, hardware/software, and supporting services.

The chief place to address this is in your overall quality planning process (Question 28). It is especially critical to consider all these elements when defining new processes, or making changes to existing ones (Questions 39–42). If you are implementing ISO 9001: 2000 for the first time (or migrating from ISO 9001: 1994), the effectiveness of your infrastructure is most likely self-evident.

Even so, you'll need to define processes for maintaining infrastructure and making changes to it as needed. Maintenance of various kinds (Question 57) and performance are all covered by other requirements of the Standard. These may be so adequately addressed in your procedures that you would not need to create a separate one for this requirement. Still, make sure that your existing system cross-references this requirement to the operational documents that address it.

ISO 9001: 2000 Requirements		
Title Facilities		
Clause 6.3	**SOP*** Recommended	**Records Required?**** No
Summary of Requirements		
The organization must identify, provide and maintain the facilities it needs to achieve the conformity of product, including: • Equipment, hardware and software. • Supporting services. • Workspace and associated facilities.		
*Question 18. **Question 22.		

ISO 9004: 2000 Guidelines—Performance Improvement
Title   Infrastructure
Clause 6.3
Summary of Guidelines

Infrastructure provides the foundation for operations and may, depending on the organization's products, include:
• Communication.
• Facilities.
• Hardware.
• Plant.
• Software.
• Support services.
• Tools and equipment.
• Transport.
• Work space.

The organization should define and provide an infrastructure in terms such as:
• Availability.
• Cost.
• Function.
• Objectives.
• Performance.
• Renewal.
• Safety.
• Security.

Uncontrollable natural phenomena may impact the infrastructure. The infrastructure plan should consider associated risks and include strategies to maintain the quality of products.

To ensure that the infrastructure continues to meet operational needs, the organization should develop and implement a maintenance approach, considering:
• Type and frequency of maintenance.
• Verification of operation of each infrastructure element, based on its criticality and usage.

The organization should also:
• Consider environmental issues associated with infrastructure, such as conservation, pollution, waste, recycling.
• Evaluate the infrastructure against the needs and expectations of all interested parties.

Transition Guidance: ISO 9001: 1994 to ISO 9001: 2000	
ISO 9001: 1994 Cross-Reference	4.1.2.2 Resources
Summary of Differences	This requirement is new.
Quality Policy Manual Updates	Add language addressing requirement to quality manual.
Procedure Updates	Recommend development of process and implementation of procedure defining the process.
See Question	99

37. Aside from human resources and infrastructure, what other types of resources are mentioned by the Standard?

CAPSULE ANSWER

The Standard provides guidelines for managing other types of resources including financial, natural, and suppliers/partnerships.

ISO 9004: 2000 *Guidelines for Performance Improvement* list *suppliers/partnerships, natural resources, and finance* as three additional categories of resources to be managed. Since there is no requirement covering these issues in ISO 9001: 2000, you are free to take or leave these guidelines. However, it is strongly recommended that you consider implementing processes for managing these resources as relevant.

Today's organizations tend to be highly dependent on the performance of suppliers and partners. More forward-looking organizations understand that variation in the performance of these entities creates needless and costly variation within their own processes. They therefore take care to (a) minimize the number of such critical relationships, and (b) manage them carefully. ISO 9001: 2000 spells out requirements for supplier control (Questions 54–56); these *Guidelines* provide additional insights on value added ways to manage such critical relationships.

Natural resources are, directly or indirectly, vital to the performance of all organizations. The *Guidelines* provided here offer suggestions for taking "preventive action" to mitigate the adverse effect of unanticipated shortages in such resources.

Financial management is a form of resource management usually conducted in accordance with fairly well defined systems. Traditionally, financial management activity has had little interface with the QMS. The *Guidelines* here point out the ways that disconnects in QMS performance can hurt financial performance. They also provide guidelines for financial management, reporting, and tying financial management generally into the QMS under the aegis of management review (Question 31).

ISO 9004: 2000 Guidelines—Performance Improvement
Title   Suppliers and partnerships Natural resources Finance
Clause 6.6 6.7 6.8
Summary of Guidelines
Organizations can benefit from establishing relationships with suppliers and partners to: • Improve processes that create value. • Promote and facilitate clear and open communication. Organizations can increase value by: • Encouraging suppliers to implement continual improvement programs and to participate in joint improvement initiatives. • Establishing two-way communication at the most appropriate levels to facilitate rapid solution of problems, and to avoid costly delays or disputes. • Evaluating, recognizing and rewarding efforts achieved by suppliers and partners. • Involving partners in identification of purchasing and joint strategy development. • Involving suppliers in the organization's design and/or development activities to share knowledge and improve the realization and delivery of conforming products.

(Continued)

- Monitoring of supplier ability to deliver conforming products.
- Optimizing the number of suppliers and partners.
- Validating supplier process capability.

Natural resources are often out of the direct control of the organization. But they can have significant positive or negative effects on its results. Organization should:

- Develop plans, or contingency plans, to ensure the resource availability and to prevent or minimize negative effects.
- Identify the natural resources that can influence organization performance.

Finance: To implement and maintain the QMS and achieve the organization's objectives, management should:

- Determine the need for, plan, make available and control financial resources.
- Develop innovative financial approaches to support and encourage improvement.

The effectiveness and efficiency of the QMS can influence the organization's financial results:

- Internally, through process and product failures, or waste in material and time.
- Externally, through product failures, costs of compensation of guarantees and warranties, costs of lost customers and markets.

Reporting of such matters may help:

- Determine ineffective or inefficient activities.
- Initiating improvement actions.

Control of financial resources should include activities for:

- Comparing actual usage against plans.
- Taking necessary action.

The financial reporting of activities related to the performance of the QMS and product quality should be used in management reviews.

38. Does the Standard impose requirements about work environment?

CAPSULE ANSWER

Your QMS must assure that no human/physical factors of the work place interfere with the process' ability to satisfy product/service requirements.

Now it does. The interesting thing is the way it defines "work environment." One might think that this would be confined to physical factors—actual working conditions. These are cited, but the Standard also includes in the work environment, an abstract—"human factors."

In essence, the Standard requires you to define and implement the "human and physical factors" of the work environment that are necessary to assure that product/service will conform to requirements. Put another way, the QMS must specify controls needed to *prevent* any human/physical factors from *interfering* with conformity of product/service.

OPPORTUNITY

Implementing ISO 9000 often creates chances to address employees' long-standing concerns about work environment.

Areas to address could include working conditions (heat, light, dust, dirt, etc.), and health and safety.

At the end of the day, quality and customer satisfaction rest in the hands of employees. Their personal satisfaction/contentment has a direct influence over their ability and willingness to see to it that customer needs are met. What control over human factors must your QMS impose to assure that product/service meets requirements? It's up to you to figure this out in your particular situation.

ISO 9001: 2000 Requirements		
Title Work environment		
Clause 6.4	**SOP*** Recommended	**Records Required?**** No
Summary of Requirements		
The organization must identify and manage the human and physical factors of the work environment needed to achieve conformity of product.		
*Question 18. **Question 22.		

ISO 9004: 2000 Guidelines—Performance Improvement
Title   Work environment
Clause 6.4
Summary of Guidelines
The organization's work environment is a combination of human and physical factors. These potentially enhance organizational performance by influencing employee: • Motivation. • Performance. • Satisfaction. Human factors affecting work environment include: • Creative work methodologies. • Ergonomics. • Opportunities for greater involvement. • Safety rules and guidance. • Special facilities for people in the organization. • Use of protective equipment. Examples of physical factors affecting work environment include: • Air flow. • Cleanliness. • Heat. • Humidity. • Hygiene. • Light. • Noise. • Pollution. • Vibration.

Transition Guidance: ISO 9001: 1994 to ISO 9001: 2000	
ISO 9001: 1994 Cross-Reference	4.1.2.2 Resources
Summary of Differences	This requirement is new.
Quality Policy Manual Updates	Add language addressing requirement to quality manual.
Procedure Updates	Recommend development of process and implementation of procedure defining the process.
See Question	99

Process Design and Improvement

39. What does the Standard say about process design?

<table>
<tr><td>CAPSULE ANSWER</td></tr>
<tr><td>You should design the processes needed to meet customer needs.</td></tr>
</table>

The Standard includes no direct requirement for process design. It does, however, provide guidelines for this in ISO 9004: 2000. These guidelines promote the concept of *improvement by means of effective process design*. The *Guidelines* are well worth implementing for your organization to achieve the Standard's overall vision of a process-based QMS.

The concept here goes to the very heart of the rationale for the organization's existence. It is intuitively obvious: the sole reason for an organization to exist is to meet the needs of one or more customers.

Doing that requires a process. Although it's intuitively obvious that one must manage these processes, the better the processes are managed, the more likely the organization is to meet customer needs consistently. Especially in industries, markets, and fields providing "parity" or "commodity" products and services. Process management is, in fact, effectively required by the Standard (Question 50).

<table>
<tr><td>PITFALL</td></tr>
<tr><td>In today's organizations, processes are often not designed. And an undesigned process is one that is very difficult to manage.</td></tr>
</table>

What hasn't been so universally recognized is the need to "design" the processes. Historically, in the typical organization, the process has not been proactively designed. The process is quite simply "the way we do things," adopted from someplace else back in dim murky memory, whipped into shape with cut-and-try trial and error, and now carried on and handed down from one generation of employees/functions to the next. Do people question the way things are done? Does anyone ever take a cold, objective, top-down, zero-based look at the process and how it works? Not usually. Because we don't have time.

OPPORTUNITY

Organizations that do a thorough analysis of existing processes often discover major opportunities to streamline, cut cost, and error-proof.

Organizations that make the time, and take the time, go on a re-markable voyage of discovery. Top management learns (often to its chagrin) just what is crawling around underneath that great big rock they think of as their processes. This may not be pleasant, but it is also not a bad thing. It is a very good thing. You can't figure out how to make things better until you clearly understand exactly how things really are.

That's what can happen when organizations fully, freely, and without reservation start implementing ISO 9001: 2000 (especially with the additional principles of ISO 9004). Defining the processes needed to meet your customers' needs (and then measuring and monitoring them—Question 41), is the first critical step toward managing the processes and continually improving them.

ISO 9004: 2000 Guidelines—Performance Improvement
Title   Product realization—issues to be considered Managing processes Process inputs, outputs, and review
Clause 7.1.2 7.1.3.1 7.1.3.2
Summary of Guidelines
The drive for continual improvement should focus on process improvement as the means by which beneficial results are achieved. Improvement of the processes will improve the QMS and the organization. Improving effectiveness and efficiency of processes can: • Improve customer satisfaction. • Increase benefits. • Reduce waste. *(continued)*

(Continued)

Identify processes needed to realize products to satisfy the requirements of customer and other interested parties. To ensure product realization, define:
- Activities.
- Control measures.
- Desired outputs.
- Equipment.
- Flows.
- Information.
- Materials.
- Methodologies.
- Other resources.
- Process steps.
- Training needs.

Define plans for process management, addressing:
- Assessment and mitigation of risks.
- Change control.
- Corrective action.
- Improvement opportunities.
- Input and output requirements such as specifications and resources.
- Process activities.
- Process analyses including operability and maintainability.
- Process validation.
- Verification of products.

To achieve improved interested-party satisfaction, define support processes and subprocesses also. Examples include:
- Availability of spare and replacement parts.
- Machining of components for assembly.
- Managing information.
- Realization of product for service.
- Training of people.

Process inputs, outputs and review

To provide a basis for the formulation of requirements to be used for verification and validation of outputs, define process inputs. These can be internal or external to the organization:
- Input derived from activities not yet fully evaluated should be subject to evaluation through subsequent review, verification and validation.
- Input requirements critical to the product or process should be identified to assign appropriate responsibilities and resources.
- Resolution of ambiguous or conflicting input requirements can involve consultation with affected internal and external parties.

(Continued)

To develop a plan for control and monitoring of the activities within the process, identify significant or critical product/process features, including:
- Competence of people.
- Documentation.
- Equipment capability and monitoring.
- Health, safety and work environment.

To satisfy customer and other interested party requirements, document and evaluate/verify process outputs against input requirements and compliance with acceptance criteria. To identify process variation, carry out product verification during operations. Evaluation should identify:
- Necessary corrective actions.
- Preventive actions.
- Potential improvements in process efficiency.

Documentation related to processes should support:
- Analysis, review and improvement of processes.
- Identification and communication of significant process features.
- Measurement and audit of processes.
- Sharing knowledge and experience in teams and work groups.
- Training in the process operation.

Evaluate the role of people within processes in order to:
- Ensure that the necessary skills exist.
- Ensure the health and safety of people.
- Promote innovation from people.
- Provide for input of people in process analysis.
- Support networks of processes.

To ensure the process is consistent with the operating plan, periodically review process performance. Consider:
- Adequacy of design and/or development outputs.
- Adequacy of design and/or development inputs.
- Consistency of inputs and outputs with planned objectives.
- Identification of and prevention against potential nonconformance.
- Potential for improvements.
- Reliability and repetitiveness of the process.
- Unresolved issues.

To achieve continual improvement and promotion of excellence throughout the organization, consider results from validation of processes and verification of outputs as process inputs.

See also Question 42—Guidelines for performance improvement (7.3.1) are applicable to process design also.

40. What does the Standard say about process validation?

CAPSULE ANSWER

Processes making product/service whose quality cannot be objectively or economically judged must be validated.

The Standard has no requirement for "process validation" per se. It is, however, strongly recommended in the *Guidelines for Performance Improvement*.

The Standard does require validation for what are sometimes called "special processes." They are processes making product/service whose quality cannot be judged objectively by any economic or convenient means. They are also processes for which problems become evident only after the customer has started using the product or service (oops!).

In manufacturing, classic examples of "special processes" include welding, soldering, and various adhesive processes. In many cases these cannot be inspected or judged without destroying the product. Virtually any verification requiring "destructive testing" may qualify as a "special process."

Special processes are also commonly found in the service arena. Typically, service is consumed at the instant it is provided, allowing no opportunity for "inspection" or "verification."

The Standard requires you to "validate" these types of processes. People working in them may require special qualifications. Specific and rigorous procedures (work instructions) may have to be developed and followed. You may need to dry-run the processes (especially service processes) under various conditions before deploying them to customers.

Although the Standard does not come right out and say you have to maintain records of process validation, it does say you have to "demonstrate" that the processes can achieve planned results. This makes records virtually mandatory.

The *Guidelines for Performance Improvement* expand considerably on process validation and offer important advice also on the need to validate process changes. The *Guidelines* also provide guidance on risk assessment.

ISO 9001: 2000 Requirements		
Title Validation of processes		
Clause 7.5.5	**SOP*** Recommended	**Records Required?**** No
Summary of Requirements		

The organization must validate any production and service processes where:
- Deficiencies may become apparent only after the product is in use or the service has been delivered.
- Output cannot be verified by subsequent measurement or monitoring processes.

Validation must demonstrate the ability of the processes to achieve planned results.

The organization must define validation arrangements that must include, as applicable:
- Qualification of equipment and personnel.
- Qualification of processes.
- Re-validation.
- Requirements for records.
- Use of defined methodologies and procedures.

*Question 18.
**Question 22.

ISO 9004: 2000 Guidelines—Performance Improvement
Title   Process validation and changes
Clause 7.1.3.3
Summary of Guidelines

At intervals appropriate to ensure timely reaction to changes impacting the process, validate products/processes to ensure products:
- Meet needs and expectations of customers.
- Satisfy other interested parties.

In particular, validate processes:
- For high-value products.
- Where deficiency in product will only be apparent in use.
- Where verification of product is not possible.
- Which cannot be repeated.

(continued)

(Continued)

Include:
- Modeling.
- Simulation.
- Trials reviews involving customers or other interested parties.

In validating products/processes, take into account:
- Disposal of the product.
- Environmental impact of the product.
- Impact of the use of natural resources including materials and energy.
- Operating conditions for the product.
- Product life-cycle.
- Qualification of equipment.
- Quality policy and objectives.
- Use or application of the product.

Implement a process change control to ensure that process changes:
- Benefit the organization.
- Satisfy the needs and expectations of interested parties.

Process changes should be:
- Controlled.
- Evaluated.
- Identified.
- Recorded.
- Reviewed.

To maintain the integrity of the product and provide information for improvement:
- Define authority for initiating change to maintain control.
- Record and communicate process changes that affect product characteristics.
- Verify product or process after any related change to ensure that the instituted change had the desired effect.

To assess the potential for the effect of possible process failures, undertake risk assessment. Use results to define and implement preventive actions to mitigate identified risks. Risk assessment tools include:
- Fault tree analysis.
- Process failure mode and effects analysis.
- Reliability assessment.
- Simulation techniques.

Transition Guidance: ISO 9001: 1994 to ISO 9001: 2000	
ISO 9001: 1994 Cross-Reference	4.9 Process control (special processes)
Summary of Differences	In essence, no different. Only addition is requirement for re-validation.
Quality Policy Manual Updates	Add re-validation language to quality manual.
Procedure Updates	Update procedure to reflect revalidation system.
See Question	100

41. Are processes subject to measurement too?

CAPSULE ANSWER

You must measure and monitor the processes needed to meet customer requirements.

Yes. Just as product and service characteristics (Question 58) and customer satisfaction (Question 65) must be measured, so too must processes.

OPPORTUNITY

Measure process outputs in terms of one or more of these dimensions: quality, time, and/or cost. Make your measurement system lean and customer-focused.

As with other measurement systems called out by the Standard, the results of this must be applied to a purpose. That purpose is "to confirm the continuing ability of each process to satisfy its intended purpose." Another way of saying: No data in a vacuum! No numbers and charts for their own sake! You're expected to gather the *right* data and measurements, analyze it, and then apply it as "lessons learned" to make things better.

This is one of several places in the Standard where some form of "process validation" is required and/or recommended (Question 40).

Though the Standard does not say so here, it would be advisable to analyze the *effectiveness* of these measurement methods every so often.

ISO 9001: 2000 Requirements		
Title Measurement and monitoring of processes		
Clause 8.2.3	**SOP*** Recommended	**Records Required?**** No
Summary of Requirements		
The organization must apply suitable methods for measurement and monitoring of those realization processes needed to meet customer requirements. These methods must confirm the continuing ability of each process to satisfy its intended purpose.		
*Question 18. **Question 22.		

ISO 9004: 2000 Guidelines—Performance Improvement
Title   Measurement and monitoring of processes
Clause 8.2.2
Summary of Guidelines
Identify measurement methods and perform measurements to evaluate process performance. Determine: • Role of measurement in process management. • Ways to incorporate measurements into the product realization process. Examples of measures of process performance include: • Accuracy. • Cost reduction. • Cycle time or throughput. • Dependability. • Effectiveness and efficiency of people. • Reaction time of processes and people to special internal and external requests. • Timeliness. • Utilization of technologies.

Transition Guidance: ISO 9001: 1994 to ISO 9001: 2000	
ISO 9001: 1994 Cross-Reference	No equivalent.
Summary of Differences	This requirement is new.
Quality Policy Manual Updates	Add language addressing requirement to quality manual.
Procedure Updates	Recommend development of process and implementation of procedure defining the process.
See Question	99

42. What about process improvement?

CAPSULE ANSWER

The *Guidance* standard includes suggestions for various process improvement methods.

The Standard has no requirement per se about improvement of process performance. It is addressed in the form of suggestions in the *Guidelines for Performance Improvement* ISO 9004: 2000. The guidelines suggest development and implementation of an *improvement process* that looks at "small step" incremental improvement (no doubt at the activity level) as well as larger scale process improvement that could include process re-engineering.

OPPORTUNITY

Management ought to be as relentless about improving processes as it usually is about improving sales and profits.

The *Guidelines* suggest also some sources of information needed to help you improve your processes.

Though these are not requirements here, improvement in general is such a recurring theme throughout ISO 9001: 2000 that a well-designed, well-implemented system will, by definition, include documented processes for process improvement.

ISO 9004: 2000 Guidelines—Performance Improvement
Title   Process for improvement
Clause 8.5.4
Summary of Guidelines
Define and implement a methodology for process improvement that can be applied to all processes and activities. Such a methodology can become a tool for improving: • Internal effectiveness and efficiency. • Satisfaction of customers and other interested parties. Examples of inputs to the improvement process include: • Financial data. • Product performance data. • Requirements and feedback from interested parties. • Service delivery data. • Test data. • Validation data. To maintain continual improvement through involvement of people, undertake small step improvement activities integral to routine operations. To achieve specific objectives, plan improvement for breakthrough projects.

Designing Products and Services

43. How must we operate our design and development process?

CAPSULE ANSWER

Your design process must be systematized, planned, and carried out under controlled conditions.

If you are a design responsible organization (and if you are not, you can exclude this requirement from your process by applying the "permissible exclusions" clause—see Question 14), you are required to operate your design process on a controlled basis as written in plans. Designs must proceed in stages as defined in the plan(s), with review and approval built into it as needed. The Standard also requires definition of responsibility and authority among groups participating in the design process, as well as effective communication among them.

OPPORTUNITY

Many design responsible organizations operate their design function as a network of personality-intensive "cottage industries." Implementing ISO 9000 allows you to systematize the design process *without* inhibiting creativity.

There is not one word in the Standard that needs to reduce, inhibit, or otherwise interfere with the creative side of design. All the Standard does is systematize the design process to assure that it proceeds in an orderly fashion—ultimately rendering designs that are consistent with customer and/or internal requirements.

Note that this requirement does not apply to your organization if you are simply modifying designs provided or created by outside entities. "Design" in the context of the Standard means that you are creating products and/or services in response to a general statement of needs or performance criteria, specified by potential customers or as part of a new market development effort. You need not (and almost certainly should not) implement a design/development control process if you are not in fact design responsible.

ISO 9001: 2000 Requirements		
Title Design and/or development planning		
Clause 7.3.1	**SOP*** Recommended	**Records Required?**** No
Summary of Requirements		

The organization must plan and control product design and/or development. Such planning must determine:
- Responsibilities and authorities for design and/or development activities.
- Review, verification and validation activities appropriate to each design and/or development stage.
- Stages of design and/or development processes.

To ensure effective communication and clarity of responsibilities, interfaces between different groups involved in design and/or development must be managed.

As the design and/or development progresses, planning output must be updated, as appropriate.

*Question 18.
**Question 22.

ISO 9004: 2000 Guidelines—Performance Improvement
Title   Design and/or development—general guidance
Clause 7.3.1
Summary of Guidelines

When designing and/or developing products and/or processes, ensure satisfaction of needs of all interested parties. Take into account:
- Dependability.
- Disposal.
- Durability.
- Environment.
- Ergonomics.
- Life cycle.
- Maintainability.
- Other risks.
- Safety.

Undertake risk assessment to identify potential for, and effect of, possible failures in products or processes. Mitigate identified risks by use results of the analysis to define and implement preventive actions.

(Continued)

Examples of tools for risk assessment of design and/or development include:
• Design failure mode and effects analysis.
• Fault tree analysis.
• Ranking techniques.
• Relationship diagrams.
• Reliability assessment.
• Simulation techniques.

Transition Guidance: ISO 9001: 1994 to ISO 9001: 2000	
ISO 9001: 1994 Cross-Reference	4.4.1 Design control—general 4.4.2 Design and/or development planning 4.4.3 Organizational and technical interfaces
Summary of Differences	Reworded, somewhat less specific, but no substantive changes.
Quality Policy Manual Updates	None needed.
Procedure Updates	None needed.
See Question	101

44. What are the requirements for design input?

CAPSULE ANSWER

You are required to define and record the objectives of the design in terms of customer needs, performance issues, and other internal and external factors.

Design input is where the design process starts. It is the pivot upon which the whole design process turns. Design input is the *definition* of the objective of the design process, expressed in terms that can later be related/compared to design output. Design input must in fact be consistent with customer needs/expectations, and/or organization needs/expectations, depending on what triggered the process in the first place.

OPPORTUNITY

Design input need not be a document. It can be, for example, a sample of some sort.

The Standard requires you to document design input in terms that are fairly specific. This is important, because design input is later compared to design output (and ultimately the final expression of the design) in various review activities. A sketch on a cocktail napkin might conceivably work, but most design input is considerably more detailed than that, especially for relatively complex and involved services and products.

You are required to review the design input and to resolve any aspect of it that is unclear, incomplete, or conflicting. You must also, for obvious reasons, keep a record of it.

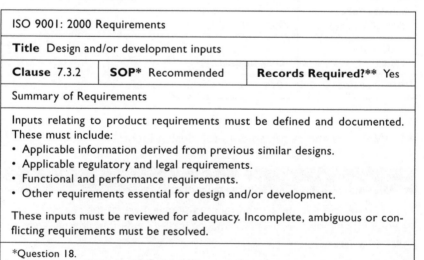

ISO 9001: 2000 Requirements		
Title Design and/or development inputs		
Clause 7.3.2	**SOP*** Recommended	**Records Required?**** Yes
Summary of Requirements		
Inputs relating to product requirements must be defined and documented. These must include: • Applicable information derived from previous similar designs. • Applicable regulatory and legal requirements. • Functional and performance requirements. • Other requirements essential for design and/or development. These inputs must be reviewed for adequacy. Incomplete, ambiguous or conflicting requirements must be resolved.		
*Question 18. **Question 22.		

ISO 9004: 2000 Guidelines—Performance Improvement
Title   Design and/or development guidance
Clause   7.3.2
Summary of Guidelines

To satisfy the needs and expectations of interested parties, identify process inputs that impact product design and/or development.

Internal inputs include:
• Dependability requirements.
• Documentation and data on existing products.
• Outputs from other processes.
• Policies.
• Skill requirements.
• Standards and specifications.

External inputs include:
• Contractual requirements and interested party specifications.
• Customer or marketplace needs and expectations.
• Industry codes of practice.
• International or national standards.
• Relevant statutory and regulatory requirements.

Take into account other inputs identify characteristics of the product or process that are crucial to its safe and proper functioning, such as:
• Disposal requirements.
• Operation, installation and application.
• Physical parameters and environment.
• Storage, handling, maintenance and delivery.

When designing/developing software and service products, inputs on end-user requirements, as well as direct customer requirements, could be particularly important. Formulate these to allow effective product testing through subsequent verification and validation.

Transition Guidance: ISO 9001: 1994 to ISO 9001: 2000	
ISO 9001: 1994 Cross-Reference	4.4.4 Design control—design input
Summary of Differences	Much more specific as to what must be documented in design input.
Quality Policy Manual Updates	Add language addressing the 4 aspects of design input now needed.
Procedure Updates	Update procedure to add specifics required in design input.
See Question	100

45. What form is required for design output?

CAPSULE ANSWER

Design output must be expressed in a way that allows comparison with design input and must be reviewed against design input to assure that it meets input requirements.

Design output is the expression of the design that is then used to facilitate the execution of the design. For products, it may be such things as blueprints, drawings, bills of material—an entire detailed package along with performance characteristics and other things. For services, it may be a collective set of procedures along with performance criteria.

PITFALL

Design output is almost always some form of document. As such, it must be placed under effective document control (Question 21).

The Standard, being generic, does not get into specifics about the form the design output must take. It simply says that design output must be expressed in a format that allows it to be verified against design input requirements (Question 44). It must cover aspects of the design that are key to safe and proper use. And it must include acceptance criteria (enabling product/service verification later).

Design output must be reviewed before release, to assure that design and/or development input requirements have been met by the design.

ISO 9001: 2000 Requirements

Title Design and/or development outputs

Clause 7.3.3	SOP* Recommended	Records Required?** Yes

Summary of Requirements

The outputs of the design and/or development process must be:
- Documented in a manner that enables verification against the design and/or development inputs.
- Approved prior to release.

Output must:
- Contain or reference product acceptance criteria.
- Define the characteristics of the product that are essential to its safe and proper use.
- Meet the design and/or development input requirements.
- Provide appropriate information for production and service operations (Question 57).

*Question 18.
**Question 22.

ISO 9004: 2000 Guidelines—Performance Improvement

Title   Design and/or development guidance

Clause 7.3.2

Summary of Guidelines

Design and/or development output should:
- Include information needed to satisfy the needs and expectations of customers and other interested parties.
- Lead to product realization.

Examples of the output of design and/or development activities include:
- Acceptance criteria.
- Methodologies.
- Product specifications.
- Purchase requirements.
- Training requirements.

Transition Guidance: ISO 9001: 1994 to ISO 9001: 2000	
ISO 9001: 1994 Cross-Reference	4.4.5 Design output
Summary of Differences	New is requirement that design output provide production/service operation information. (This was always implicit before; now it is explicit.)
Quality Policy Manual Updates	Add new requirement.
Procedure Updates	Update procedure to reflect additional requirement.
See Question	100

46. Are we supposed to review the designs?

CAPSULE ANSWER

At defined points during the design process, you must carry out reviews to assess the adequacy of the design and to examine and deal with problems that may have arisen.

The Standard requires that designs be reviewed "at suitable stages." Objectives of the review are: to assess the extent to which the design meets quality requirements (i.e., customer and internal requirements), and to identify, and propose solutions for, any problems related to the product or service being designed.

OPPORTUNITY

Designs undergo many reviews, most of them informal. There is no need to formalize every single review that happens. Specify intervals in each design project where *formal* reviews will take place, and then carry those out on a documented basis.

You are required to include in the review(s)—there can be, and often are, more than one—all functions involved in the design stage being reviewed. This can include customers.

You are required to record the results of design reviews as well as any follow-on actions that may take place.

Overall, design review is an activity intended to assure that the design, as it emerges, conforms with the requirements defined by (or on behalf of) customers or the organization itself. It is also aimed at facilitating communication among the functions involved, assuring—at least hopefully—a relatively smooth process toward design of a product/service that meets or exceeds all requirements.

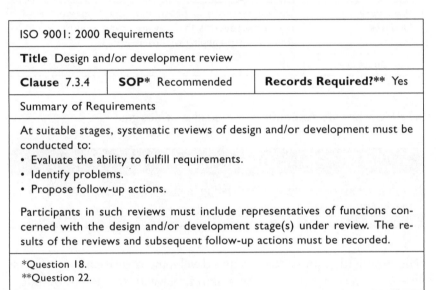

ISO 9001: 2000 Requirements		
Title Design and/or development review		
Clause 7.3.4	**SOP*** Recommended	**Records Required?**** Yes
Summary of Requirements		
At suitable stages, systematic reviews of design and/or development must be conducted to: • Evaluate the ability to fulfill requirements. • Identify problems. • Propose follow-up actions. Participants in such reviews must include representatives of functions concerned with the design and/or development stage(s) under review. The results of the reviews and subsequent follow-up actions must be recorded.		
*Question 18. **Question 22.		

ISO 9004: 2000 Guidelines—Performance Improvement
Title   Design and/or development review
Clause 7.3.3
Summary of Guidelines
Conduct periodic reviews of design and/or development objectives, including: • Evaluation of potential hazards or modes of failure in product use. • Life-cycle data on performance of the product. • Meeting verification and validation goals. • Potential impact of the product on the environment. To satisfy the needs and expectations of interested parties, undertake reviews of design and/or development outputs, as well as the process. Verify that outputs meet the design specifications and validate that they meet customer needs.

Transition Guidance: ISO 9001: 1994 to ISO 9001: 2000	
ISO 9001: 1994 Cross-Reference	4.4.6 Design review
Summary of Differences	More specific about what the review must cover. Records must now include follow-up actions.
Quality Policy Manual Updates	Add language calling out the required specifics.
Procedure Updates	Update system and procedure to reflect what standard now requires that review cover, as well as additional record-keeping requirements.
See Question	100

47. How are we to confirm the quality of designs?

CAPSULE ANSWER

You must carry out design verification to confirm the conformity of design output with design input.

The Standard requires "design and development verification." This is in essence a comparison of the design input with the design output—a one-for-one matching to confirm that the results of the design meet, at least in theory, the requirements posed by design input.

Usually this comes toward the end of the formal design process. The idea is to catch design problems while the design is in a more or less theoretical stage, before things have gone "live" with prototype testing, often done for products; or dry run/piloting activities, often done for new services (Question 48).

You must record the results of design verification, as well as any new activities that may arise as a result of it (redesign, etc.).

ISO 9001: 2000 Requirements		
Title Design and/or development verification		
Clause 7.3.5	**SOP*** Recommended	**Records Required?**** Yes
Summary of Requirements		
Design and/or development verification must be performed to ensure the output meets the design and/or development inputs. The results of the verification and subsequent follow-up actions must be recorded.		
*Question 18. **Question 22.		

ISO 9004: 2000 Guidelines—Performance Improvement
Title   Design and/or development review
Clause 7.3.3
Summary of Guidelines
To enable design and/or development methodologies and decisions to be reviewed, generate sufficient data through verification and validation activities. The review of methodologies should include: • Failure investigation activities. • Future design and/or development process needs. • Process and product improvement. Examples of verification activities include: • Comparative methodologies, such as alternative design and/or development calculations. • Evaluation against similar products. • Testing, simulations or trials to check compliance with specific input requirements.

Transition Guidance: ISO 9001: 1994 to ISO 9001: 2000	
ISO 9001: 1994 Cross-Reference	4.4.7 Design verification
Summary of Differences	Shortened; guidance note was removed. No substantive impact.
Quality Policy Manual Updates	None needed.
Procedure Updates	None needed.
See Question	101

48. What else must we do to confirm design quality?

CAPSULE ANSWER

You must carry out design validation to "test" the product/service in quasi real-life conditions, before delivering/implementing product/service.

Design validation is usually some form of prototype testing (products) or dry run/piloting activity (services). It is a test of the design under more or less "real" operating conditions. The purpose is to see how well the designed product/service meets the needs, expectations, and specifications of customers, usually as outlined in design input (Question 44).

Validation is a flat-out requirement. Even when full validation cannot be undertaken before delivery of product or implementation of service, the Standard requires you to validate to the greatest extent practical. You must also record validation results, as well as the results of any follow-up activities that may be warranted.

OPPORTUNITY

Prevention is an "upstream" activity. The further upstream in the process that you place your controls, the less they tend to cost, and the more effective they tend to be.

Design validation is just another way of assuring that customers experience only the refined product or service that is consistent with their needs or expectations. It is truly a preventive activity: It not only protects the customer, it protects your organization, too. It is one more way (design verification—Question 47—is another) for you to be sure your design "hits the mark" before you invest resources in full-bore delivery. It is easier and less expensive to correct design problems uncovered at design verification than it is after the product and/or service is fully deployed.

ISO 9001: 2000 Requirements		
Title Design and/or development validation		
Clause 7.3.6	**SOP*** Recommended	**Records Required?**** Yes
Summary of Requirements		

To confirm that resulting product is capable of meeting the requirements for the intended use, design and/or development validation must be performed.

Wherever applicable, validation must be completed before the delivery or implementation of the product. Where it is impractical to perform full validation before delivery or implementation, partial validation must be performed to the extent applicable.

The results of the validation and subsequent follow-up actions must be recorded.

*Question 18.
**Question 22.

ISO 9004: 2000 Guidelines—Performance Improvement
Title   Design and/or development review
Clause 7.3.3
Summary of Guidelines

To enable design and/or development methodologies and decisions to be reviewed, generate sufficient data through verification and validation activities. The review of methodologies should include:
• Failure investigation activities.
• Future design and/or development process needs.
• Process and product improvement.

Partial validation of the design and/or development outputs may be needed to provide confidence in their future application, by validating:
• Direct customer services before widespread introduction.
• Engineering designs before construction, installation or application.
• Software outputs before installation or use.

Transition Guidance: ISO 9001: 1994 to ISO 9001: 2000	
ISO 9001: 1994 Cross-Reference	4.4.8 Design validation
Summary of Differences	More stringent and specific. New is requirement that validation be completed before product delivery or implementation; and that partial validation must be performed where total validation cannot be done on time. Records requirement is new also.
Quality Policy Manual Updates	Add language addressing new requirements.
Procedure Updates	Update system and procedure to reflect new requirements.
See Question	100

49. How must we handle design changes?

CAPSULE ANSWER

Before a change is implemented, it must be reviewed, approved, and recorded by authorized people with full consideration of change's potential impact.

Design changes must be reviewed—and approved—by people in authority, *before* the changes are implemented.

This is nothing surprising and nothing new from ISO 9001: 1994. What is new is that the review must consider the effects the changes could conceivably have on things such as (1) interaction of component parts of the product/service; (2) impact on existing products/services.

PITFALL

When there are noncompliances in the design phase, they are most often found in the design change process.

The change review/approval must be recorded. So must any follow-up actions that the review may necessitate.

ISO 9001: 2000 Requirements		
Title Control of design and/or development changes		
Clause 7.3.7	**SOP*** Recommended	**Records Required?**** Yes
Summary of Requirements		

Design and/or development changes, including evaluation of the effect of changes on constituent parts and delivered products, must be:
- Controlled.
- Documented.
- Identified.

The changes must be:
- Approved (as appropriate) before implementation.
- Validated.
- Verified.

The results of the review of changes and subsequent follow-up actions must be documented.

*Question 18.
**Question 22.

ISO 9004: 2000 Guidelines—Performance Improvement
Title None
Clause None
Summary of Guidelines
No specific guidelines offered. See Questions 46–48.

Transition Guidance: ISO 9001: 1994 to ISO 9001: 2000	
ISO 9001: 1994 Cross-Reference	4.4.9 Design changes
Summary of Differences	Change control requirement is new. So is requirement that evaluation look at the effect of changes. Record-keeping requirement is new also.
Quality Policy Manual Updates	Update to include added requirements.
Procedure Updates	Update system and procedure to reflect new requirements.
See Question	100

Meeting Customer Needs

50. How does the Standard address process management?

CAPSULE ANSWER

The Standard requires you to plan and document your "realization" processes that contribute toward meeting customer needs.

ISO 9001: 2000 is structured around concepts of process management. The focus is at the very first requirement under Section 7 (product and/or service realization). This requires you to identify, plan, document, and implement the "sequence and interaction of processes" that result in products and/or services that meet customer needs. (It helps, incidentally, if there is also a proactive effort to *design* the processes. See Question 39.)

Each process plan must include defined objectives, acceptance criteria, definition of processes, documentation (including records), resources, facilities, and verification/validation measures.

Note that the requirement applies to "realization" processes only. The guidelines for performance improvement recommend applying the same control principles to "support" processes. These are processes that do not necessarily impact the customer directly, and are not necessarily value-adding (in the direct sense), but that have a major impact on the organization's overall ability to meet customer needs.

ISO 9001: 2000 Requirements		
Title Planning of realization processes		
Clause 7.1	**SOP*** Required	**Records Required?*** Yes
Summary of Requirements		

Product realization is that sequence of processes and sub-processes required to achieve the product. Planning of the realization processes must be:
- Consistent with the other requirements of the organization's QMS.
- Documented in a form suitable for the organization's method of operation.

In planning product realization processes, the organization must determine the following, as appropriate:
- Acceptance criteria.
- Quality objectives for the product, project or contract.
- records that are necessary to provide confidence of conformity of the processes and resulting product.
- The need to establish processes and documentation, and provide resources and facilities specific to the product.
- Verification and validation activities.

*Question 18.
**Question 22.

ISO 9004: 2000 Guidelines—Performance Improvement
Title Product realization—general guidance
Clause 7.1
Summary of Guidelines

Each organization is a network of interdependent processes. These processes occur in two types:
- Realization processes—produce the organization's products that, in turn, add value to the organization.
- Support processes—including management processes, are necessary to the organization, but do not directly add value.

Realization and support processes can include networks of sub-processes.

Each process is made up of three elements:
- Inputs.
- Activities.
- Outputs.

To ensure all processes operate as an efficient system, the organization should:
- Recognize that the output of one process is often the input to another.
- Apply process management principles to all activities.

Transition Guidance: ISO 9001: 1994 to ISO 9001: 2000	
ISO 9001: 1994 Cross-Reference	4.9 Process control
Summary of Differences	This requirement is new.
Quality Policy Manual Updates	Add language addressing requirement to quality manual.
Procedure Updates	Recommend development of process and implementation of procedure defining the process.
See Question	99

51. Does the Standard make any mention of communicating with customers?

CAPSULE ANSWER

The Standard requires you to manage your process for customer communication—including product information as well as gathering feedback.

The Standard in fact requires that you implement a defined process covering your customer communications activities.

OPPORTUNITY

Here for the first time the ISO 9000 Standard specifically affects the advertising/public relations function(s) of the organization.

The requirement provides for two way communication: from you to customers (product/service information, responding to inquiries, etc.), and from customers to you (product/service feedback, customer complaints). The overall aim of the communication process is to improve your ability to meet customer needs.

The *Guidelines for Performance Improvement* extends the concept to communication with interested parties beyond your customer base.

It recommends developing a process for communicating with those other groups about their needs and expectations.

ISO 9001: 2000 Requirements		
Title Customer communication		
Clause 7.2.3	**SOP*** Recommended	**Records Required?**** No
Summary of Requirements		
The organization must identify and implement arrangements for customer communication relating to: • Contracts (including changes). • Customer feedback, including customer complaints. • Inquiries. • Order handling. • Product information.		
*Question 18. **Question 22.		

ISO 9004: 2000 Guidelines—Performance Improvement
Title   Processes related to interested parties
Clause 7.2
Summary of Guidelines
Define, implement and maintain processes to ensure adequate understanding of the needs and expectation of interested parties. These processes: • Could actively involve customers and other interested parties.   • Should include identification and review of relevant information.   Examples of information sources include results from: • Benchmarking.   • Competitor analysis.   • Contract requirements.   • Market research.   • Processes due to statutory or regulatory requirements.   • Processes or activities specified by the customer or other interested parties.   Maintain full understanding of the process requirements of the customer, or other interested party, before taking action to comply. This understanding and its impact should be mutually acceptable to the participants.

Transition Guidance: ISO 9001: 1994 to ISO 9001: 2000	
ISO 9001: 1994 Cross-Reference	4.3 Contract review
Summary of Differences	This requirement is new.
Quality Policy Manual Updates	Add language addressing requirement to quality manual.
Procedure Updates	Recommend development of process and implementation of procedure defining the process.
See Question	99

52. What must we do to identify our customers' requirements?

CAPSULE ANSWER

Your process must determine what *all* your customer's needs are—general and specific, spoken and unspoken.

You must establish a process for identifying customer requirements. But the requirement does not begin and end simply with what the customer *tells* you he or she wants. And it is not enough simply to track the "intrinsic" characteristics of the product and/or service the customer says he or she wants. The Standard also requires that you determine requirements beyond these, such as: (1) requirements related to fitness for intended purpose and (2) legal and regulatory requirements. Requirements the customer makes tacitly and does not necessarily articulate to you.

In this, ISO 9001: 2000 goes well beyond requiring a "review" of the customer's requirements (although that too is required—Question 53). The Standard requires that you have and maintain a thorough understanding of *all* the customer's requirements: stated and unstated. This is, after all, the first step in meeting their needs—you can't possibly expect to do that if you don't know what they are!

ISO 9001: 2000 Requirements		
Title Identification of customer requirements		
Clause 7.2.1	**SOP*** Recommended	**Records Required?**** No
Summary of Requirements		
The organization must determine customer requirements including: • Product requirements specified by the customer, including requirements for availability, delivery, and support. • Product requirements not specified by the customer but necessary for intended or specified use. • Obligations related to product, including regulatory and legal requirements.		
*Question 18. **Question 22.		

ISO 9004: 2000 Guidelines—Performance Improvement
Title Processes related to interested parties
Clause 7.2
Summary of Guidelines
See Question 50.

Transition Guidance: ISO 9001: 1994 to ISO 9001: 2000	
ISO 9001: 1994 Cross-Reference	4.3 Contract review
Summary of Differences	This requirement is new.
Quality Policy Manual Updates	Add language addressing requirement to quality manual.
Procedure Updates	Recommend development of process and implementation of procedure defining the process.
See Question	99

53. What steps should we take to review customer requirements?

CAPSULE ANSWER

You must review customer orders before acceptance to assure that all requirements are clear, complete, and unambiguous, and that you have the capability to meet requirements.

You must review customer requirements *before* accepting/processing the customer order (or a change to a customer order). The review must also assess requirements that are pertinent to the order and set by you—but that may not be mentioned by the customer.

The review must also assure that you have the ability to meet all the requirements. By accepting the order, you are attesting that you have that capability.

The Standard further requires you to resolve any unclear or questionable order issues before proceeding with processing the order.

OPPORTUNITY

This is another upstream, prevention-oriented requirement. Because if you slip up here, it does not matter how good your process is down the line—you've already blown it.

This requirement, which also appeared pretty much intact in ISO 9001: 1994, has to do with the review of *specific customer orders*. Another requirement, new to ISO 9001: 2000 (Question 52), requires you to operate an overall process for determining customer needs, whether stated or unstated.

The requirement also requires a bit of regimentation and discipline among those tasked with sales functions. This can conflict with the "get the order at all costs" philosophy of high-achieving marketing people. There are often cases in which sales/marketing people routinely write flawed, incomplete, or downright misleading orders under the philosophy of "let the home office take care of this." Such people need to make a psychological shift to a philosophy of "do it right the first time"—thereby *preventing* problems that can crop up later, not only for the "home office" but for themselves, too.

All subsequent quality efforts, and efforts to meet customer needs, begin with doing this one with consistent and persistent excellence. If there is an optimal place for a zero defects philosophy to take root, it is here. Because if you misunderstand customer requirements at this stage, downstream you'll have to work very hard and at great expense to rework and redo—costing you money *and* adversely affecting the customer.

ISO 9001: 2000 Requirements		
Title Review of product requirements		
Clause 7.2.2	**SOP*** Recommended	**Records Required?**** Yes
Summary of Requirements		
Before committing to supply a product to the customer, the organization must review: • Identified customer requirements. • Additional requirements determined by the organization. This review must ensure that: • Product requirements are defined. • Contract or order requirements differing from those previously expressed (e.g., in a proposal, quotation, etc.) are resolved. • Customer requirements are confirmed before acceptance (especially where customer provides no documented statement of requirement). • Organization has the ability to meet defined requirements. The results of the review and subsequent follow-up actions must be recorded. Where product requirements are changed, the organization must ensure that: • Relevant documentation is amended. • Relevant personnel are made aware of the changed requirements.		
*Question 18. **Question 22.		

ISO 9004: 2000 Guidelines—Performance Improvement
Title   Processes related to interested parties
Clause 7.2
Summary of Guidelines
See Question 50.

Transition Guidance: ISO 9001: 1994 to ISO 9001: 2000	
ISO 9001: 1994 Cross-Reference	4.3 Contract review
Summary of Differences	Besides customer requirements, organization must now review requirements that it determines. Review of contract changes must now be recorded, and documentation relevant to the change must be updated.
Quality Policy Manual Updates	Add language reflecting new requirements.
Procedure Updates	Update system and procedure to reflect new requirements.
See Question	100

54. What must we do to control our purchasing processes?

CAPSULE ANSWER

You must implement a process for selecting and controlling suppliers of products and services that affect your "realization processes," your final product/service, and your customers.

The Standard requires you to control the process you use for purchasing products and services that affect your "realization processes" and their output. The greater the impact a purchased/product has on your process and/or your customers, the stricter the controls must be.

This starts with the method you use for selecting suppliers/ vendors. "Let your fingers do the walking" may work some places, but the Standard requires you to have an evaluation process that assures that suppliers can meet your requirements. The evaluation process must include criteria for evaluation and selection. The Standard does not specify what the criteria must be. It certainly does not require that your suppliers be compliant to ISO 9001: 2000 or any other standard. It's up to you to set the criteria, develop the evaluation and selection system, implement it, and stick to it.

You must also keep records of supplier evaluations and any related follow-up actions.

The Standard also has rules governing the purchasing process itself (Question 55) and verifying purchased products/services (Question 56).

OPPORTUNITY

A well-run purchasing process is the ultimate "upstream" strategy and takes the concept of "prevention" to a new dimension.

The better job you do here, the easier time you will have controlling your own process, minimizing variation, and efficiently meeting the needs of your customers. "Garbage in" doesn't necessarily mean "garbage out" but the principle of GIGO has some realism behind it—"garbage in" costs you money to fix. With so many options available for so many types of supplied products and services, why should you put up with anything less than optimal performance from your suppliers? *You're the customer!*

ISO 9001: 2000 Requirements		
Title Purchasing control		
Clause 7.4.1	**SOP*** Recommended	**Records Required?**** Yes
Summary of Requirements		
To ensure purchased product conforms to requirements, the organization must control its purchasing processes. The type and extent of control must be dependent upon the effect of purchased product on subsequent realization processes and their output. The organization must: • Define criteria for supplier selection and periodic evaluation. • Evaluate and select suppliers based on their ability to supply product consistent with the organization's requirements. • Record results of evaluations and follow-up actions.		
*Question 18. **Question 22.		

ISO 9004: 2000 Guidelines—Performance Improvement
Title   Purchasing process   Suppliers
Clause   7.4.1   7.4.2
Summary of Guidelines

To ensure that purchased products satisfy needs and requirements of the organization and its interested parties, identify and implement processes for selection, evaluation control of purchased products. These processes should include:

- Assessment of risks associated with the purchased product.
- Contract administration.
- Identification of needs.
- Inquiries, quotations and tendering.
- Nonconforming purchased products.
- Ordering.
- Purchase documentation.
- Selection of suppliers, including those with unique processes.
- Supplier control and supplier development.
- Total cost of purchased product (taking account of performance, price and delivery).
- Verification of purchased products.

Establish processes to identify potential suppliers or to develop existing suppliers and evaluate their ability to supply the required products. These processes may include:

- Audits of supplier management systems.
- Checking references for customer satisfaction.
- Evaluation of relevant experience.
- Evaluation of supplier potential capability to provide the required products efficiently and within schedule.
- Financial assessment to assure the viability of the supplier throughout the intended period of supply.
- Logistic capability including locations and resources.
- Review of product quality, price, delivery performance and response to problems.
- Service and support capability.

To benefit from available specialist knowledge, develop process requirements and specifications with suppliers. Involve them also in the specification of QMS requirements relating to their products.
See Question 37.

Transition Guidance: ISO 9001: 1994 to ISO 9001: 2000	
ISO 9001: 1994 Cross-Reference	4.6.1 Purchasing—general 4.6.2 Purchasing—evaluation of subcontractors
Summary of Differences	New is requirement for periodic evaluation of suppliers. Record-keeping requirement is also new, technically (although 1994 was often interpreted as requiring these types of records).
Quality Policy Manual Updates	Add language addressing new requirements.
Procedure Updates	Update system and procedure to reflect new requirements.
See Question	100

55. Must we use any special purchasing documents?

CAPSULE ANSWER

Purchasing documents must include an adequate level of detail as to the product/service ordered. They must also be reviewed for adequacy before release.

The Standard does not require any particular purchasing documents. It does require that purchasing documents that you use include clearly detailed information. This covers descriptions of product/service ordered, as well as any particular procedures or processes required.

PITFALL

While designing and implementing your purchasing process, it is easy to overlook people who have purchasing authority—especially those in middle management line and production positions.

Your process must also assure that the requirements specified in purchasing documents are adequate. Therefore, you must designate the functions with responsibility and authority and ensure that they document their approval wherever it is needed.

In most organizations, this requirement is not a huge problem. There are organizations, though, whose purchasing processes are somewhat informal. There are also organizations that operate two purchasing systems: the official one, well documented—and the real one, which everyone understands but which has never been written down. Implementing a system compliant with ISO 9001: 2000 can often be an opportunity to get everyone on the same page.

ISO 9001: 2000 Requirements		
Title Purchasing information		
Clause 7.4.2	**SOP*** Recommended	**Records Required?**** No
Summary of Requirements		
Purchasing documents must contain information describing the product to be purchased, including where appropriate QMS requirements as well as requirements for approval or qualification of: • Equipment. • Personnel. • Procedures. • Processes. • Product. Before release of purchasing documents, the organization must ensure the adequacy of specified requirements.		
*Question 18. **Question 22.		

ISO 9004: 2000 Guidelines—Performance Improvement

Title   Suppliers

Clause 7.4.2

Summary of Guidelines

Ensure that orders for purchased product are adequate to satisfy the input requirements of the organization's processes. Consider these issues:
• Acceptance criteria.
• Communication.
• Documentation and records.
• Logistic requirements.
• Preservation of product.
• Product identification.
• Purchasing from qualified suppliers.
• Right of access to supplier's premises.
• Traceability of product.

Establish a process to verify purchased products for compliance with specification. Vary verification activity level according to:
• Historical performance of the supplier.
• Nature or the type of product.

Define the need for records of:
• Purchased product verification.
• Response to nonconformity reports.
• Supplier communication.

Transition Guidance: ISO 9001: 1994 to ISO 9001: 2000	
ISO 9001: 1994 Cross-Reference	4.6.3 Purchasing data
Summary of Differences	Reworded; less specific; no substantive changes.
Quality Policy Manual Updates	None needed.
Procedure Updates	None needed.
See Question	101

56. What must we do to verify the quality of purchased products and/or services?

CAPSULE ANSWER

You must specify and implement measures sufficient to verify that supplied product/service meets requirements.

All the Standard says here is that the arrangements for verifying purchased products/services must be identified and implemented. So there must be some arrangements for this—you simply need to specify what they are.

OPPORTUNITY

If you have vendors with particularly strong and consistent controls, such that you virtually never experience quality problems with them, you can place them in a vendor classification that *exempts* you from having to verify their quality. This is virtually mandatory if you are drop-shipping from vendor to your customer.

This requirement is cross-referenced with 8.2.4 (Measurement and monitoring of product and/or service—Question 58). That is where the details of measurement and so on are expressed, replacing what used to be called "inspection and testing." Essentially, you need to implement verification measures sufficient to assure that purchased product/service meets requirements. This may mean 100 percent inspecting, for critical products/services supplied by really bad suppliers; or zero verification, for suppliers with excellent and proven quality systems and controls, and/or supplying products or services with little impact on your process, product/service, or customers.

The Standard also mentions the possibility of you, or your customer, verifying supplier quality at *their* location. Should you or the customer require this, the Standard requires that you indicate this in your purchasing documents.

ISO 9001: 2000 Requirements		
Title Verification of purchased product		
Clause 7.4.3	**SOP*** Recommended	**Records Required?**** No
Summary of Requirements		

The organization must identify and implement the activities necessary to verify purchased product.

Where the organization or its customer proposes to perform verification activities at the supplier's premises, the organization must specify in the purchasing information:
• Intended verification arrangements.
• Method of product release.

*Question 18.
**Question 22.

ISO 9004: 2000 Guidelines—Performance Improvement
Title   Verification of purchased product
Clause None
Summary of Guidelines

No specific guidelines. See questions 54 and 55.

Transition Guidance: ISO 9001: 1994 to ISO 9001: 2000	
ISO 9001: 1994 Cross-Reference	4.6.4 Verification of purchased product
Summary of Differences	Reworded and melted down. The awkward language about "verification by the customer" has (thankfully) been removed. No substantive changes.
Quality Policy Manual Updates	None needed.
Procedure Updates	None needed.
See Question	101

57. What are the requirements for production of product and/or service?

CAPSULE ANSWER

You are required to plan and control production and service operations, including those done after initial delivery.

As in ISO 9001: 1994, this "process control" element requires that processes for production of product be planned and controlled. Like the former Standard, this requirement spells out various subprocesses that are required, including specifications, work instructions, and appropriate and maintained equipment. Unlike the former Standard, the requirement now includes *service* operations as well as production operations.

PITFALL

Work instructions are a traditional cause of money-guzzling bloat. Keep the population small; keep their length lean; involve process owners in writing them.

The requirement for work instructions specifically says "where necessary." Period. Work instructions are for activities that are "critical" to the achievement of product/service conformity. Therefore not *every* work process or task needs to be spelled out in a work instruction. Do not overdocument! Use informed judgment.

Though the requirements do not mention it here, *process validation* and control of process changes are central to process control. See Question 40.

ISO 9001: 2000 Requirements		
Title Operations control		
Clause 7.5.1	**SOP*** Recommended	**Records Required?*** No
Summary of Requirements		

The organization must control production and service operations through:
- Availability and use of measuring and monitoring devices.
- Availability of information that specifies product characteristics.
- Availability, where necessary, of work instructions.
- Implementation of defined processes for release, delivery and applicable post-delivery activities.
- Implementation of monitoring activities.
- Use and maintenance of suitable equipment for production and service operations.

*Question 18.
**Question 22.

ISO 9004: 2000 Guidelines—Performance Improvement
Title Operations and realization
Clause 7.5.1
Summary of Guidelines

Identify requirements for operations that realize products or deliver services to:
- Ensure compliance with specifications.
- Satisfy the needs and expectations of interested parties.

To meet these needs and expectations, review and consider:
- Ability to comply with contractual requirements.
- Automation.
- Capacity planning.
- Communication.
- Electronic monitoring.
- Intended use.
- Logistics.
- Post-realization activities.
- Preservation.
- Problem prevention.
- Product flow and yield.
- Relevant statutory and regulatory requirements.
- Training and competence of people.
- Training required.

To maintain operational capability, appropriately maintain and adequately protect the infrastructure during and between uses.

Transition Guidance: ISO 9001: 1994 to ISO 9001: 2000	
ISO 9001: 1994 Cross-Reference	4.9 Process control—general 4.19 Servicing
Summary of Differences	Service is now included in this requirement. The language is much more straightforward and generic. (Validation—"Special processes"—is now addressed by requirement 7.5.5; see Question 40.) No substantive changes.
Quality Policy Manual Updates	None needed.
Procedure Updates	None needed.
See Question	I0I

58. Are we required to inspect and test product and/or service?

Capsule Answer

You must have a recorded system for verifying that product and/or service meets customer and internal requirements.

Inspect and test may not be the correct terms. A better one is *verification*. You are required to implement a system to verify that the product and/or service you make meets product requirements. This is an umbrella term for (1) customer requirements, and (2) your own internal requirements. To do this, you have to document the acceptance criteria—in other words, write down (or otherwise quantify) what "good" is. You have to produce evidence that you are doing the measuring and monitoring. And you have to keep records.

Previous versions of the Standard used the terms *inspection and testing*. The 1994 Standard was very specific about various levels—

incoming inspection, in-process inspection, final inspection. This specificity is gone. The Standard now uses the deceptively generic term *appropriate*. You still have to have a system for measuring and monitoring product and service to assure that customer and internal requirements are being met—and you must be able to prove that it works.

The key here is not to go overboard. Measures such as verification are reactive, not proactive. The more you can do upstream in the process to minimize variation and foolproof the production tasks, the less need there is for burdensome (and nonvalue-added) verification activities. The Standard is more than agreeable to measures such as these (the Standard being, as it is, huge on prevention versus detection). Unfortunately, inspection and testing are easy, and require little thought, and are therefore the default measures even when other, much less costly and much more proactive measures, could be developed.

ISO 9001: 2000 Requirements		
Title Measurement and monitoring of product		
Clause 8.2.4	**SOP*** Recommended	**Records Required?**** Yes
Summary of Requirements		
To verify that product requirements are met, the organization must, at appropriate stages of product realization: • Measure and monitor product characteristics. • Document evidence of conformity with acceptance criteria. Records must indicate authority responsible for product release. Unless otherwise approved by customer, product release and service delivery must not proceed until all specified activities have been satisfactorily completed.		
*Question 18. **Question 22.		

ISO 9004: 2000 Guidelines—Performance Improvement

Title   Measurement and monitoring of product

Clause 8.2.3
           7.6

Summary of Guidelines

To verify conformance to specified requirements:
- Establish and specify product measurement requirements (including acceptance criteria).
- Plan and perform product measurement.

In choosing a product measurement methodology, consider:
- Characteristics to be measured at each point.
- Conformance to specified requirements of its products, and those provided by suppliers.
- Customer established points for witness or verification of selected product characteristics.
- Documentation and acceptance criteria to be used.
- Equipment and tools required.
- Final inspections to confirm that all specified inspections and testing are completed and accepted.
- Inspections or testing that are required to be witnessed or performed by statutory and regulatory authorities.
- Location of each measurement point in its process sequence.
- Outputs of measurement process of product.
- Qualification of material, product, process, people or QMS.

Consider also where, when and how organization intends, or is required by customer or statutory and regulatory authorities, to engage qualified third parties to perform:
- In-process inspections or testing.
- Product verification.
- Product validation.
- Type testing.

Perform product measurement prior to delivery to verify that product conforms to requirements. Review product measurement approaches, and records of verification. Make appropriate improvement.

Typical examples of product measurement records include:
- Certificates as required.
- Electronic data.
- Inspection and test reports.
- Material release notices.

To minimize the need for measurement and monitoring activities and devices, eliminate potential errors from processes via "fool-proofing" means.

Transition Guidance: ISO 9001: 1994 to ISO 9001: 2000	
ISO 9001: 1994 Cross-Reference	4.10 Inspection and testing
Summary of Differences	Serious meltdown from existing requirement. Gone is much of the widget-maker specificity. In essence, requirement is no less strict and no different from ISO 9001: 1994.
Quality Policy Manual Updates	None needed.
Procedure Updates	None needed.
See Question	101

59. What are the requirements for identification and traceability?

> ## CAPSULE ANSWER
> You are required to identify product/service by suitable means and in terms of verifications it has undergone.

In general, the Standard requires objective means for various kinds of identification of products and/or services while they are under your control.

> ## OPPORTUNITY
> For most organizations, the "suitable means" for identification already exist. Implementation is simply a matter of codifying it and making sure it is consistently practiced.

You must first of all identify product and/or service "by suitable means" throughout the processes. This should include component parts, where their interaction can affect conformity to requirements. This requirement is one of the extremely intuitively obvious ones. One seldom sees a process utterly lacking in identification methods. More frequently, identification methods are undocumented and/or inconsistently applied.

<table>
<tr><td align="center">PITFALL</td></tr>
<tr><td>The inspection/test/verification status of product/service is almost always very informal and people-dependent—and a cause of major customer-affecting problems.</td></tr>
</table>

You must also identify product and/or service in terms of (1) what verification activities it has undergone, and (2) the results of those verification activities. In other words, if your plan calls for product to be inspected or service to be verified at certain points, then there needs to be an objective method of knowing, for each "unit" in the process, whether it has undergone prescribed inspections and what the outcomes of the inspections were. This can be done with records, signage, "travelers," or by designated/objectively marked location. This requirement is not hard to meet, but is usually not effectively met by organizations that have not implemented good ISO 9001: 2000 systems.

Traceability is not required by the Standard. Where it is otherwise required, the Standard requires you to maintain records of the unique identification of product and/or service.

ISO 9001: 2000 Requirements		
Title Identification and traceability		
Clause 7.5.2	**SOP*** Recommended	**Records Required?**** Yes
Summary of Requirements		
Where appropriate, the organization must identify the product by suitable means throughout production and service operations. The organization must: • Control and record the unique identification of the product, where traceability is a requirement. • Identify the status of the product with respect to measurement and monitoring requirements.		
*Question 18. **Question 22.		

ISO 9004: 2000 Guidelines—Performance Improvement
Title   Identification and traceability
Clause 7.5.2
Summary of Guidelines
To satisfy customer and other interested party requirements for control of products, establish a process and documentation for identification and traceability. The need for this may be due to: • Contract requirements. • Hazardous materials. • Intended use of application. • Relevant statutory and regulatory requirements. • Risk mitigation. • Status of products, including component parts.

Transition Guidance: ISO 9001: 1994 to ISO 9001: 2000	
ISO 9001: 1994 Cross-Reference	4.8 Product identification and traceability 4.12 Inspection and test status
Summary of Differences	Only change is that what was once two elements are now combined into one. No other substantive changes.
Quality Policy Manual Updates	None needed.
Procedure Updates	None needed.
See Question	100

60. How are we to handle customer property?

CAPSULE ANSWER

While customer property is entrusted to you, you must treat it with care.

The way you normally would, even if ISO 9001: 2000 did not tell you: with care. That's how you must treat all customer property while you are using it or otherwise controlling it. In an unusual burst of prescriptiveness, the Standard goes on to require you to identify, verify, store, and maintain the property; and to record and report to the customer any of its property found to be lost, damaged, or otherwise unsuitable.

Do not be too quick to assume that your organization does not handle customer property. It is in fact rare to find an organization that does not. Customer property frequently includes things such as tooling, test equipment, packaging, dunnage, or labeling. It can include raw material provided to you for processing and return. It can include components furnished to you for assembly into kits. It can even include intellectual property, such as customer confidential information.

Note also that there are service operations for whom customer property is the very warp and woof of their business. These include equipment repair operations of various kinds. In these cases, the documented processes for operations control (Question 57) may effectively cover the requirements called for here. Check to be sure.

ISO 9001: 2000 Requirements		
Title Customer property		
Clause 7.5.3	**SOP*** Recommended	**Records Required?**** Yes
Summary of Requirements		
The organization must exercise care with customer property while it is: • Being used by the organization. • Provided for incorporation into the product. • Under the organization's control. The organization must identify, verify, protect and maintain customer property. Such property that is lost, damaged or otherwise found to be unsuitable for use must be recorded and reported to the customer.		
*Question 18. **Question 22.		

ISO 9004: 2000 Guidelines—Performance Improvement
Title   Customer property
Clause 7.5.3
Summary of Guidelines
Identify responsibilities for the protection of the value of customer owned property and other assets owned by customers and other interested parties while under the organization's control. Examples: • Customer materials handled by service operations such as storage. • Information provided in confidence. • Ingredients or components supplied for inclusion in a product. • Intellectual property, including specifications, drawings, and so on. • Packaging materials supplied by the customer. • Product supplied for repair, maintenance or upgrading. • Services supplied on behalf of the customer such as transport of customer property to a third party.

Transition Guidance: ISO 9001: 1994 to ISO 9001: 2000	
ISO 9001: 1994 Cross-Reference	4.7 Control of customer supplied product
Summary of Differences	Essentially the same. Only substantive change is that the clause now applies to customer property "provided for use," over and above what is provided by customers for inclusion in product. (The 1994 Standard was frequently interpreted this way, however.) Caution that organization must "exercise care" is actually redundant to other language in the clause. Definition of intellectual property as "customer property" is in a note, and affirms a long held interpretation.
Quality Policy Manual Updates	If system does not address customer property provided for use (besides incorporation), add this language to quality manual.
Procedure Updates	Update procedure as needed.
See Question	100

61. What controls are we required to have for handling, packaging, storage, preservation, delivery?

CAPSULE ANSWER

Your processes for identifying, handling, packaging, storing, preserving, and delivering product/service must not affect conformity to requirements.

Interestingly, the Standard does not speak so much about "controls" in these areas. They are not required to "conform" to anything. What the Standard requires you to do is "preserve" conformity to customer requirements during all phases of operations, both internal and external. This applies not only to the treatment of "complete" products and services, but also to the handling of components or service stages.

PITFALL

Organizations with traditional quality control orientation often overlook the processes such as these that take place *after* the product itself has been created. Yet here is where organizations without appropriate systems and controls often snatch defeat from the jaws of victory.

This sounds generic, but it is in fact generality with teeth. You still need to define processes in these areas and conform to them. Otherwise, you have no way of assuring that the processes will not hurt conformity to customer requirements. You therefore need to spell out approved "best practices" for identification, handling, packaging, storage, preservation, and delivery of product and/or service.

ISO 9001: 2000 Requirements

Title Preservation of product

Clause 7.5.4	**SOP*** Recommended	**Records Required?*** No

Summary of Requirements

The organization must preserve conformity to customer requirements of product, and constituent product parts, during:
- Internal processing.
- Delivery to the intended destination.

This must include:
- Handling.
- Identification.
- Packaging.
- Protection.
- Storage.

*Question 18.
**Question 22.

ISO 9004: 2000 Guidelines—Performance Improvement

Title   Preservation of product

Clause 7.5.4

Summary of Guidelines

For handling, packaging, storage, preservation and delivery, define and implement processes designed, during internal processing, final product delivery, and throughout product life cycle, to prevent:
- Damage.
- Deterioration.
- Misuse.

Consider the need for any special requirements arising from the nature of the product associated with:
- Electronic media.
- Hazardous materials.
- Materials that are unique or irreplaceable.
- Software.
- Specialist personnel products.

Communicate information to interested parties about resources needed to preserve product.

Transition Guidance: ISO 9001: 1994 to ISO 9001: 2000	
ISO 9001: 1994 Cross-Reference	4.15 Handling, storage, packaging, preservation, and delivery
Summary of Differences	Colossal meltdown. Requirement has been rendered much more brief and generic, but is really no less strict. Only substantive change is that requirement applies not only to product, but also to "constituent parts" of product.
Quality Policy Manual Updates	Add language about constituent parts as needed.
Procedure Updates	Update procedure(s) to address constituent parts as needed.
See Question	100

62. How should we control measuring and testing equipment?

CAPSULE ANSWER

You must verify/calibrate all devices used to check product/service, or monitor their production, to provide confidence in the measurement/ monitoring results.

You must implement a process that assures that measuring and monitoring devices are measuring/monitoring the way you expect them to (i.e., accurately). This sounds simple. In practice it can be quite complicated. This requirement has traditionally caused more grief (all of it avoidable) than just about any other.

OPPORTUNITY

One way to reduce the cost of calibrating/verifying seldom used devices is to *not* calibrate them until they are actually needed. In the meantime, keep them secured (locked away) so they cannot be mistaken for "legal" devices.

First of all, a measuring and monitoring device is: (1) Any device or instrument that is used to check or measure a product/service characteristic to check its conformity to a defined goal or standard. Examples of these can include linear measuring devices (rulers, tape measures, etc.); more esoteric devices (micrometers, calipers, depth gauges, scales, spectrometers, software programs); and custom-made testing devices (forms, jigs, etc.). (2) Any device or instrument that controls the production of key product/service characteristics (e.g., variable machine controls, computerized controls).

Pitfall

Don't overlook common measuring devices such as tape measures, rulers, and so on. If these are used to verify product/service conformance anywhere in the production cycle, they must be controlled.

The way to avoid problems and to meet the requirements fully is to do your homework, develop a calibration/checking process, and follow it faithfully. Start by identifying all the critical product/service characteristics you are measuring and/or controlling. For each, determine:

- The device you'll use to measure or monitor it.
- The device's "unique identifier" (serial number or other ID).
- The accuracy needed.
- The method you'll use to check or calibrate the device. Many firms contract with external calibration services. Others have their own in-house calibration processes.
- The "traceability" of the calibration. You'll need to check or calibrate the device with equipment that is *itself* checked/calibrated, with "traceability" (in the form of documentation) to national or international standards. Most commonly in the United States this means standards maintained by the National Institute of Standards and Technology (NIST). Where no such traceability exists, then you need to document the "basis" for the calibration (i.e., controlled prints or drawings of custom forms, fixtures, jigs).
- The calibration frequency. For devices that are seldom or lightly used, it may be practical to calibrate before every use. Otherwise, establish set intervals, defaulting to manufacturer recommendations, where they exist. Then you can adjust the frequency based on actual use and experience. It is very common for firms to calibrate *more often* than is justifiable by experience.

PITFALL

Most organizations verify/calibrate more often than they need to. This is a waste of resources. Let your experience with each device guide you when you set the intervals. Be prepared to show evidence to justify the interval that you set.

■ The method used to display calibration status. It is highly advisable to mark/label the device itself with the date last calibrated and the date next due, so that people using the device know they are using an "approved" one.

OPPORTUNITY

This is yet another chance to "declutter" your operation. Get rid of unneeded or redundant measuring devices.

Most often, firms doing their own calibration/verification write work instructions governing how it is done. *Complete* records of calibration need to be maintained. Employees must use equipment in a manner that does not harm its ability to measure accurately. Finally, if, upon calibration/verification, you find that a device has not been measuring accurately—and this could have an adverse effect on customers—you must take appropriate action to recheck the validity of tests made with the suspect device and/or advise customers of a potential problem.

A good solid calibration/verification system is one of the best preventive actions you can implement. It gives you and your customers confidence in the measurements and tests you are doing. (If you don't have confidence in the measurements and tests, why bother doing them?) What brings firms to grief in this area can be:

■ Not including all measurement/monitoring devices used to check product/service and/or control the production of product/service. (If you're going to err here, err on the side of putting *too many* in rather than leaving some out.) For example, some firms leave out *employee-owned* measurement equipment—these *must* be included as well.

■ Not having calibration traceability.
■ Failing to keep complete records.

ISO 9001: 2000 Requirements		
Title Control of measuring and monitoring devices		
Clause 7.6	**SOP*** Recommended	**Records Required?**** Yes
Summary of Requirements		

To assure conformity of product to specified requirements, the organization must identify:
• The measurements to be made.
• The measuring and monitoring devices required.

Measuring and monitoring devices must be used and controlled to ensure that measurement capability is consistent with the measurement requirements. Where applicable, measuring and monitoring devices must:
• Be calibrated and adjusted periodically or prior to use, against devices traceable to international or national standards. Where no such standards exist, the basis used for calibration must be recorded.
• Be safeguarded from adjustments that would invalidate the calibration.
• Be protected from damage and deterioration during handling, maintenance and storage.
• Have the results of their calibration recorded.
• Have the validity of previous results re-assessed (and corrective action taken) if devices are subsequently found to be out of calibration.

Software used to measure and monitor specified requirements must be validated prior to use.

*Question 18.
**Question 22.

ISO 9004: 2000 Guidelines—Performance Improvement
Title   Control of measuring and monitoring devices
Clause 7.6
Summary of Guidelines

Where measuring and monitoring devices are used for verification, ensure that they are:
• Calibrated.
• Maintained to accepted standards, giving confidence to the results.

Transition Guidance: ISO 9001: 1994 to ISO 9001: 2000	
ISO 9001: 1994 Cross-Reference	4.11 Control of inspection, measuring, and test equipment
Summary of Differences	Main change is that requirement specifically addresses monitoring as well as measuring devices. (1994 was often interpreted this way.) Otherwise language is more generic and straightforward, with no other substantive changes.
Quality Policy Manual Updates	Update to include monitoring devices as needed.
Procedure Updates	Change system and procedure(s) to address monitoring devices as needed.
See Question	100

Measuring and Improving

63. Why a whole section devoted to measurement, analysis, and improvement?

CAPSULE ANSWER

The measurement, analysis, and improvement section of the Standard requires the application of tools for assessing process performance in many key areas and applying lessons learned to continuous improvement.

The systems required by Section 8 of ISO 9001: 2000 close the loop. Unlike the 1994 version of the Standard, which was huge on reactive measures (inspection and testing), took a swipe at prevention, and gave data gathering and analysis the shortest shrift, ISO 9001: 2000 requires strong processes that (1) gather data about QMS performance, customer satisfaction, and other critical indicators; (2) analyze the data; and (3) apply lessons learned to process improvement.

The old Inspection and Testing (4.10) requirement is virtually gone in its previous form—the most significant "meltdown" in the new

Standard. Now, the Standard requires specific systems for measuring and monitoring not only product/service characteristics (which echoes the old Inspection and Testing model), but also QMS performance, customer satisfaction, and process performance.

Included here are familiar processes for assessment and improvement: internal audit, corrective action, preventive action. And all of it is pulled together under a new requirement for *continuous improvement* of the quality system by means of an overall measurement, analysis, and improvement process that takes into account the results of *all* of the subsystems called out here.

ISO 9004: 2000 Guidelines—Performance Improvement
Title   Measurement, analysis, and improvement—general guidance
Clause 8.1.1
Summary of Guidelines
Provide at appropriate intervals for the measurement and evaluation of: • Customer satisfaction. • Items required by other interested parties. • Process capability. • Product. Determine the need for the use of statistical techniques for analyzing data, including verifying process operations and product characteristics: • Select statistical techniques that are suitable for the application. • Control and monitor their use. Relevant data needed to monitor and improve the organization's performance should be: • Analyzed. • Collected. • Communicated. • Recorded. • Summarized. Measurements should not be purely for the accumulation of information. They should generate appropriate action. Therefore: • Define measurement criteria and objectives. • Deploy measurements only where the benefit can be identified. • Evaluate measurements in terms of the added value provided to the organization. The results of measurement can show a level of achievement, but examine trends and variation also. Identify and understand their causes.

64. What are the general requirements for measurement, analysis, and improvement?

> ## CAPSULE ANSWER
>
> You must implement a thorough system for measurement and data analysis that drives continual improvements to the QMS and processes for producing product and/or service.

You must define and document (figure out and write down) processes for measuring things, generating data, and then analyzing data so that you can make positive use of it. Areas to measure include:

- How satisfied customers are (Question 65).
- How well the QMS is performing (Question 57).
- How well the processes of producing and delivering products/ services are performing.
- How consistently product/service characteristics meet requirements (as defined by your customer and/or by you) (Question 58).

This is more than just inspection and testing. More than simple statistical techniques. You are required to close the loop—with a vengeance. All in the aid of assuring that we know, at all times, the extent to which our process is helping us to meet customer needs.

Two other important points. To keep the measurement/analysis system from becoming an orphan, the *Guidelines for Performance Improvement* suggest that the *effectiveness* of measurement methods be regularly checked. This is one way of keeping firms from producing numbers for numbers' sake—a common pitfall in quality management. In addition, the results of these activities should be an input to the management review process. This in effect "forces" management to at least become aware of critical measurements—to face the news, good or bad. When continually aware of facts backed by data, management tends to make better decisions.

For expanded detail on the various measurement, analysis, and improvement processes that are required, see the other entries for Section 8.

ISO 9001: 2000 Requirements		
Title Planning		
Clause 8.1	**SOP*** Recommended	**Records Required?**** No
Summary of Requirements		
The organization must define, plan and implement the measurement and monitoring activities needed to assure conformity and achieve improvement. This includes determination of the need for, and resulting use of, applicable methodologies including statistical techniques.		
*Question 18. **Question 22.		

ISO 9004: 2000 Guidelines—Performance Improvement
Title   Measurement, analysis improvement—issues to be considered
Clause 8.1.2
Summary of Guidelines
Use measurement and analysis to establish appropriate improvement priorities for the organization and to generate involvement of all interested parties: • Clearly define the purpose of all measurements and analysis. • Review measurements periodically. • Verify data continually for accuracy and completeness. Implement appropriate tools to communicate information resulting from measurement and analyses. Measure effectiveness of communication to interested parties to determine whether the information is clearly understood. As an improvement tool, benchmark individual processes and customer satisfaction.

Transition Guidance: ISO 9001: 1994 to ISO 9001: 2000	
ISO 9001: 1994 Cross-Reference	4.20 Statistical techniques
Summary of Differences	Seriously reworded. Requirement that measurement/ monitoring activities be defined, planned, and implemented is new. So is requirement that these activities (including statistical techniques) address improvement (not just process capability and product characteristics).
Quality Policy Manual Updates	Update quality manual language to address expanded scope.
Procedure Updates	Update procedure(s) to cover scope of measurement and monitoring activities.
See Question	100

65. How are we supposed to track customer satisfaction?

CAPSULE ANSWER

You must measure and monitor customer satisfaction.

You must have a methodology (another word for process) for monitoring customer satisfaction and dissatisfaction. The Requirement itself is fairly bare-bones. But it can cause headaches for organizations that have had no defined processes in this area. Even many more advanced organizations have problems tracking customer *dissatisfaction*—let alone satisfaction! Yet the Standard requires that you track and analyze both aspects.

For help, look to the *Guidelines for Performance Improvement* (ISO 9004). The guidelines encourage you to systematically gather and analyze information of all types on customer satisfaction—thereby drawing closer to your customers and equipping yourself to anticipate and meet their needs earlier, and more fully, than your competitors.

ISO 9001: 2000 Requirements		
Title Measurement of customer satisfaction		
Clause 8.2.1	**SOP*** Recommended	**Records Required?**** No
Summary of Requirements		
As one of the measurements of QMS performance, the organization must monitor information on customer satisfaction and/or dissatisfaction. The methodologies for obtaining and using this information must be determined.		
*Question 18. **Question 22.		

ISO 9004: 2000 Guidelines—Performance Improvement
Title   Measurement of customer satisfaction
Clause 8.2.1
Summary of Guidelines
There are many sources of customer-related information. Examples include: • Customer requirements and contract information. • Feedback on all aspects of product. • Information relating to competition. • Market needs. • Service delivery data. Identify internal and external sources of written and verbal customer and end-user information: • Establish processes to gather, analyze, and deploy this information. • Specify the methodology and the measures to be used and the frequency of gathering and analyzing data for review. • Plan data collection methodologies. The process for requesting, measuring and monitoring feedback of customer satisfaction and dissatisfaction should provide information on a continual basis. It should address: • Conformance to requirements. • Meeting needs and expectations of customers. • Price and delivery of product. Examples of sources of information on customer satisfaction include: • Customer complaints. • Direction communication with customers. <div align="right">*(continued)*</div>

(Continued)

- Focus groups.
- Questionnaires and surveys.
- Reports in various media.
- Reports from consumer organizations.
- Sector studies.

Establish and use sources of customer satisfaction information. Cooperate with customers to anticipate needs. To efficiently obtain the "voice of the customer," establish processes for implementing appropriate marketing activities.

Transition Guidance: ISO 9001: 1994 to ISO 9001: 2000	
ISO 9001: 1994 Cross-Reference	No equivalent.
Summary of Differences	This requirement is new.
Quality Policy Manual Updates	Add language addressing requirement to quality manual.
Procedure Updates	Recommend development of process and implementation of procedure defining the process.
See Question	99

66. We must measure customer satisfaction. Must we also measure the satisfaction of any other groups?

> ## CAPSULE ANSWER
>
> The "Guidelines for Performance Improvement" suggest that you implement a system to measure the satisfaction of groups, such as employees, that are critical to your success.

There is no such *requirement*. But the *Guidelines for Performance Improvement*, ISO 9004: 2000, suggests quite specifically that you implement a system to measure the satisfaction of other stakeholders. This includes employees, owners, suppliers, and society.

Though this is not a requirement, the guidance ought to be taken seriously and implemented as appropriate. Especially important is the satisfaction of *employees*. They are the process owners; it is in their hands that quality and customer satisfaction ultimately rest.

ISO 9004: 2000 Guidelines—Performance Improvement
Title   Measurement and monitoring of satisfaction of interested parties
Clause 8.2.4
Summary of Guidelines
Identify measurement information needed to meet needs of other interested parties at appropriate stages of product realization. With respect to needs of people: • Assess individual and collective performances and their contribution to organizational results. • Gather opinion regarding ways that organization satisfies their needs and expectations. With respect to needs of owners: • Assess capacity to attain defined goals. • Identify value contributed by actions taken. • Measure impact of external factors on results. • Measure financial performance. With respect to needs of suppliers: • Measure or monitor quality of product purchased. • Measure performance of purchasing processes of organization. • Monitor supplier performance and their compliance with purchasing policy. With respect to needs of society: • Define appropriate measurements relative to its objectives, for interaction with society. • Periodically assess efficiency of its actions and perceptions of results by relevant parts of society.

67. Are other measurement/monitoring methods mentioned by the Standard?

CAPSULE ANSWER

Linking business measures to QMS activity, and self-assessing to other non-ISO criteria, are suggested by the ISO 9004 guidelines for performance improvement.

Yes, but they are not requirements. The ISO 9004: 2000 *Guidelines for Performance Improvement* recommend that you link business financial measures to the QMS as part of your effort to improve the process. In addition, various self-assessment strategies are suggested. An Annex to the Guidelines provide a self-assessment approach. You may also wish to assess your organization to various national quality awards criteria (i.e., Malcolm Baldrige National Quality Award). These come under the heading of *guidance only* and are not requirements.

OPPORTUNITY

This is yet another chance for you to unite the quality system with your other business processes—an outstanding strategy to assure its continued viability.

ISO 9004: 2000 Guidelines—Performance Improvement
Title   Financial approaches   Self-assessment
Clause 8.2.1.4   8.2.1.5
Summary of Guidelines
Evaluate and establish methods to communicate QMS results throughout the organization in financial terms. Provide such information for management review for planning and implementing the improvement of processes and activities. Examples of financial approaches are: • Costs of conformance and nonconformance. • Life-cycle approach. • Prevention, appraisal and failure costs analysis. Consider also establishing and implementing a self-assessment process, consistent with organization's objectives and priorities. Methodology should focus on determining the degree of efficiency and effectiveness of implementation of the QMS defined in the International Standard. It should: • Be easy to understand and to use. • Have minimal impact on the use of management resources. • Help to determine priorities. • Not be considered as an alternative to internal or external quality auditing. • Provide input for identifying areas in the organization requiring improvement. • Provide an overall view of the performance of the organization and the degree of maturity of the QMS. • Provide input to enhance the performance of the organization's QMS.

68. Are we required to audit ourselves?

CAPSULE ANSWER

You must audit your quality system on a scheduled, recorded basis, to assure that it is well implemented and in compliance with the Standard.

You must carry out "objective" audits of your quality management system (QMS) to make sure the QMS meets the requirements of the Standard and is working effectively. You must follow a written procedure that spells out the audit process, responsibilities, schedule, recording/reporting processes, and so on.

OPPORTUNITY

A well-run internal audit system is a powerful aid to management decision making, because audit results are based on objective evidence.

Objective means that audits must be done by people who are independent of the work they are auditing. It is highly recommended that you select your audit team from a cross-section of the levels and functions of the organization. Subcontracting of the internal audit process is permitted by certain registrars, but this is not recommended.

Audit frequency should be varied from section to section, and based on the importance of the activity being audited and results of past audits of the activity. You must record results of internal audits, and report them to management. Though this particular requirement does not mention it, you are also required to take action to fix deficiencies uncovered by audits. The best mechanism for this is corrective action (Question 72).

PITFALL

Internal audit must never become an adversarial, disciplinary tool.

Internal audit is one of the four self-reinforcement mechanisms of the ISO 9000 system. Internal audit is also the most potent force for implementing the new QMS. No matter how carefully and thoroughly you document your processes, a well-planned and aggressively conducted internal audit program will (a) act as a teaching tool to educate the workforce on the QMS, and (b) highlight aspects of the process(es) and the QMS that are not well thought out or well implemented.

For details on designing and running an effective internal audit program, see Questions 84 to 86.

ISO 9001: 2000 Requirements		
Title Internal audit		
Clause 8.2.2	**SOP*** Required	**Records Required?**** Yes
Summary of Requirements		

The organization must conduct periodic internal audits to determine whether QMS:
- Conforms to requirements of this International Standard.
- Has been effectively implemented and maintained.

Organization must define audit:
- Frequency.
- Methodology.
- Program.
- Scope.

The organization's audit plan must take into consideration:
- Results of previous audits.
- Status and importance of activities and areas to be audited.

Audits must be conducted by personnel other than those who perform activity being audited.

A documented procedure must include:
- Assurance of audit independence.
- Recording results.
- Reporting to management.
- Responsibilities and requirements for conducting audits.

Management must take timely corrective action on deficiencies found during audit.

Follow-up actions must include:
- Verification of implementation of corrective action.
- Reporting of verification results.

*Question 18.
**Question 22.

ISO 9004: 2000 Guidelines—Performance Improvement
Title Internal audit
Clause 8.2.1.3
Summary of Guidelines

Establish an internal audit process to:
* Assess QMS strengths and weaknesses.
* Review efficiency/effectiveness of other organization activities and support processes.

Internal audit process should include:
* Follow-up activities.
* Implementation.
* Planning.
* Reporting.

To permit changes based on findings and observations obtained during audit, planning should be flexible. In developing internal audit plans, obtain input from:
* Area to be audited.
* Other interested parties.

Internal auditing should also consider:
* Adequacy and accuracy of performance measurement.
* Analysis of quality cost data.
* Assigned responsibilities and authorities.
* Capability of processes.
* Competence of people.
* Documentation of results.
* Effective implementation of processes.
* Existence of adequate documentation.
* Identification of nonconformance.
* Improvement activities.
* Opportunities for improvement.
* Performance results and expectations.
* Relationships with interested parties, including internal customers.
* Use of information technology.
* Use of statistical techniques.

Besides documenting nonconformances, internal audit reporting should also indicate:
* Areas for improvement (with recommendations).
* Areas of outstanding performance.

Follow-up activities include:
* Verification of implementation.
* Timeliness and effectiveness of corrective action.
* Effectiveness of internal audit process.

Transition Guidance: ISO 9001: 1994 to ISO 9001: 2000	
ISO 9001: 1994 Cross-Reference	4.17 Internal quality audits
Summary of Differences	More succinct and straightforward. New is requirement that audits check compliance to the International Standard. New also is requirement that audits check for effective implementation and maintenance of the QMS.
Quality Policy Manual Updates	Revise language to include new requirements.
Procedure Updates	Update system and procedure to reflect new requirements.
See Question	100

69. How must we handle nonconforming product or service?

CAPSULE ANSWER

You must implement a system that to the greatest extent possible prevents nonconforming product/service from affecting the customer—and results in controlled correction.

You must implement a system that prevents the "unintended use or delivery" of product and/or service that does not meet customer or internal requirements.

PITFALL

When nonconformities occur, organizations often fail to deploy the first and most important reactive measure: *mitigation*—prompt action to reduce or eliminate any adverse effect on the customer.

The first goal here is to *protect the customer*—to prevent or mitigate damage or harm to the customer resulting from nonconforming product or service. You are also required to correct the problem. This should be via repair (rendering the product/service useful, if not necessarily to original specification), rework (restoring to original specification), or discard. The Standard requires *reverification* of product/service that is repaired or reworked, before providing it to the customer; this important step is often overlooked.

In a further measure for customer protection, the Standard requires also that you take "appropriate action regarding consequences of nonconformity" when the nonconformity is found after product/service delivery. In other words, when product/service does not meet customer requirements, you're expected to make it right.

You may also obtain "concession" from the customer (or regulatory body, where appropriate) for acceptance of off-spec product or service. This means that the customer knows what the actual condition is; knows that the product/service does not fully meet requirements, but is willing to accept it anyway. In these cases, the actual condition of the product/service must be recorded.

OPPORTUNITY
Be sure to apply disciplined corrective/preventive action to all instances of product/service nonconformity, especially those that affect customers directly.

We'd like to *prevent* nonconformities from happening in the first place. ISO 9001: 2000 puts prevention before detection. But let's face it: nonconforming products and services are facts of life in a world in which perfection is a goal, not a norm. Further, we are expected to learn from such situations and (by implementing corrective/preventive actions) keep them from recurring.

ISO 9001: 2000 Requirements

Title Control of nonconformity

Clause 8.3	**SOP*** Recommended	**Records Required?**** Yes

Summary of Requirements

The organization must ensure, via a documented procedure, that product that does not conform to requirements is:
- Identified.
- Controlled to prevent unintended use or delivery.

Nonconforming product must be:
- Corrected.
- Subjected to re-verification to demonstrate conformity.

When nonconforming product is detected after delivery or use has started, organization must take appropriate action regarding consequences of nonconformity.

It will often be required that proposed rectification of nonconforming product be reported for concession to:
- Customer.
- End-user.
- Regulatory or other body.

*Question 18.
**Question 22.

ISO 9004: 2000 Guidelines—Performance Improvement

Title   Control of nonconformance

Clause 8.3

Summary of Guidelines

People at all process stages should have authority to report nonconformances, especially people engaged in:
- Monitoring processes.
- Verifying output.

Prompt attention to nonconformances permits prompt corrective action. To maintain achievement of product requirements:
- Control product identification, segregation and disposition to prevent misuse.
- Define authority for reaction to nonconformances.

(continued)

(Continued)

To help learning and provide data for analysis and improvement activities, record all nonconformances and their disposition. Consider recording information on nonconformances corrected in normal course of work. Such data can provide valuable process improvement information.

Define a process for review and disposition of all nonconformances. Designated persons should review to identify trends or patterns of occurrence. Trends should be:
• Input to management review.
• Subject to corrective action.

People carrying out review should:
• Be competent to evaluate effects of nonconformance.
• Have authority and resource to define corrective action.

Customer acceptance of disposition may be a contractual requirement.

Transition Guidance: ISO 9001: 1994 to ISO 9001: 2000	
ISO 9001: 1994 Cross-Reference	4.13 Control of nonconforming product
Summary of Differences	Seriously shortened and rendered more generic and less specific. New is the requirement that you "take appropriate action regarding consequences of nonconformity" when nonconformity is found after customer receives product. Another substantive addition is that proposed fix of nonconforming product may have to be reported to a "regulatory body or other body" besides the end-user. This particular statement is so tentatively worded so as to render it almost meaningless.
Quality Policy Manual Updates	Update to specifically address the two changes above.
Procedure Updates	Document process for correcting nonconformity found after product is received or service has begun.
See Question	100

70. What must we do with data that we collect?

CAPSULE ANSWER
Collected data must be analyzed to identify improvement opportunities, system trends, customer satisfaction/dissatisfaction—leading to continuous improvement.

Having established measurement points, we must now, according to the Standard, actually *collect and use* the data. By doing this we are required to track important aspects of quality such as customer satisfaction, improvement opportunities, trends, and the effectiveness of the QMS. This should lead us to continually improve all aspects of our process and our system. Good data provides the basis upon which to take meaningful action.

PITFALL
Perpetual motion can be defined as a report or statistical analysis, requested by persons long gone for reasons long forgotten, that continues to be produced, month after month.

This requirement is to further draw us away from that old "quality control" bugaboo of data for its own sake. It's a good idea to periodically review the types of data being gathered and the applicability of the analyses that are deployed. Such things tend over time to become etched in stone and performed by rote, mindlessly gobbling up time and attention long after their purpose is forgotten and usefulness has faded.

ISO 9001: 2000 Requirements		
Title Analysis of data		
Clause 8.4	**SOP*** Recommended	**Records Required?**** No
Summary of Requirements		

The organization must collect and analyze appropriate data to:
• Determine QMS suitability and effectiveness.
• Identify improvements that can be made.

This includes data generated by:
• Measuring and monitoring activities.
• Other relevant sources.

The organization must analyze this data to provide information on:
• Characteristics of processes, product and their trends.
• Conformance to customer requirements.
• Customer satisfaction and/or dissatisfaction.
• Suppliers.

*Question 18.
**Question 22.

ISO 9004: 2000 Guidelines—Performance Improvement
Title   Analysis of data for improvement
Clause 8.4
Summary of Guidelines

Analyze data from various sources to:
• Assess performance against plans and goals.
• Identify areas for improvement.

To help assess, control, and improve process performance, analyze data using statistical methodologies. This may require analysis of:
• Product specifications.
• Relevant processes, operations and quality records.

To evaluate overall organization performance, integrate and analyze Information and data from all parts of the organization. Present analyses in a format that is suitable to different levels of management.

Use results of analysis to:
• Assess organization effectiveness and efficiency.
• Assess operational performance.

(Continued)

- Benchmark process performance.
- Check customer satisfaction and dissatisfaction.
- Determine cause of problems.
- Determine economics of quality and financial and market-related performance.
- Guide effective corrective and preventive action trends.
- Identify supplier contribution.
- Identify satisfaction level of other interested parties.

Transition Guidance: ISO 9001: 1994 to ISO 9001: 2000	
ISO 9001: 1994 Cross-Reference	No equivalent.
Summary of Differences	This requirement is new.
Quality Policy Manual Updates	Add language addressing requirement to quality manual.
Procedure Updates	Recommend development of process and implementation of procedure defining the process.
See Question	99

71. What overall approach does the Standard take on the issue of improvement?

CAPSULE ANSWER

You are required to continually improve the QMS via a defined process that coordinates internal audit, management review, corrective action, and so on.

First of all, you are *required* to improve the QMS. Continually. This requirement, new in ISO 9001: 2000, requires a process that pulls together traditional ISO 9000 elements: corrective and preventive action, management review, internal audit, and so on. The process must use the results of these activities to effect QMS improvement.

What's good about this is that a responsible person in the organization must now be tasked with coordinating these monitoring and analysis efforts and drawing meaningful conclusions from them. No longer will management review, internal audit, and so on, operate in isolated chimneys. With a strong overall perspective that a coordinating process will bring, chronic and systemic and repeating problems will have a better chance of being identified, isolated, and eliminated.

This requirement serves also as an umbrella for several other more specific, operational requirements, such as corrective/preventive action (Questions 72–73) and internal audits (Question 68).

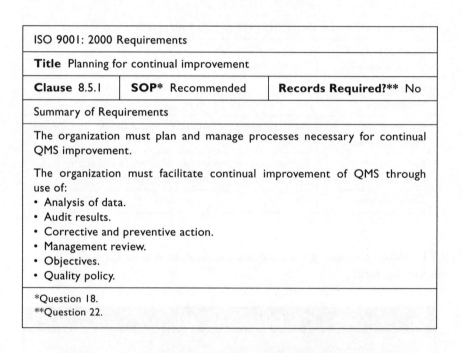

ISO 9001: 2000 Requirements		
Title Planning for continual improvement		
Clause 8.5.1	**SOP*** Recommended	**Records Required?**** No
Summary of Requirements		
The organization must plan and manage processes necessary for continual QMS improvement. The organization must facilitate continual improvement of QMS through use of: • Analysis of data. • Audit results. • Corrective and preventive action. • Management review. • Objectives. • Quality policy.		
*Question 18. **Question 22.		

ISO 9004: 2000 Guidelines—Performance Improvement	
Title	General guidance—introduction Improvement—general
Clause	8.1.1 8.5.1

Summary of Guidelines

Rather than wait for a problem to reveal improvement opportunities, continually seek to improve processes. Potential improvements can range from continual activities to long-term improvement projects. Put in place a process in place to identify and manage improvement projects.

Continual improvement requires more than just measurement. Improvement requires change within organization. Measurement itself does not initiate change.

To continually improve:
- Continually monitor and record implementation actions, to provide data for future improvements.
- Plan implementation of improvement actions.
- Promote use of creative and innovative approaches for improvement processes.
- Provide adequate resources.
- Set realistic and challenging goals.

Measurements of improvement efforts should be taken for a clearly defined purpose. Use collected information and data throughout organization to support effective and efficient management. Identification of causes of deviations may result in changes to:
- Processes.
- Product.
- QMS.

Results of analysis of data from improvement activities should be one of inputs to management review (Question 31).

Transition Guidance: ISO 9001: 1994 to ISO 9001: 2000	
ISO 9001: 1994 Cross-Reference	No equivalent.
Summary of Differences	This requirement is new.
Quality Policy Manual Updates	Add language addressing requirement to quality manual.
Procedure Updates	Recommend development of process and implementation of procedure defining the process.
See Question	99

72. What does "corrective action" mean?

CAPSULE ANSWER

Corrective action prevents recurrence of nonconformities by identifying and eliminating their root causes.

Corrective action is reactive. As the term implies, it is about fixing problems *after* they have occurred. The Standard is quite specific as to the purpose—"to prevent recurrence of nonconformities"—and the basic method: "by eliminating their causes." It is one of the most powerful and easy to implement tools for improvement in the ISO 9000 system.

PITFALL

Some organizations, who (in error) regard corrective action as a "negative" activity, try to minimize it by restricting the types of problems that employees can report. This is a grievous and potentially fatal mistake.

The defined process must provide for identification of nonconformities and determination of their causes. This means *root* causes. The whole secret of effective corrective action is taking the time and implementing the discipline to identify root causes, not just symptoms or effects.

Corrective action ought to be applied to any kind of quality related problem: customer complaints, product/service nonconformities, process disconnects/bottlenecks, as well as the ever-annoying chronic or repeating hiccups, glitches, and headaches that cause the expenditure of untold resources for fire fighting. Management discretion can and should be applied. Management has to deploy its resources wisely in all areas of the organization, not just corrective action.

Corrective action is also applied against deficiencies raised in internal audits (Question 68).

OPPORTUNITY

Analyzing corrective action by tallying causes and looking for commonalities is a highly effective and beneficial "big picture" activity that organizations lacking a disciplined corrective action system miss out on.

The Standard also requires (as it did in 1994) that a review take place to assure that corrective action is taken and has been effective. This vital step is often overlooked, requirements notwithstanding. Or it is often done slap-dash without any real study. A strong tool to implement in your corrective action system is a periodic review of problems *and causes* to look for "repeaters"—sure signs that the actual root causes are not being effectively dealt with.

ISO 9001: 2000 Requirements		
Title Corrective action		
Clause 8.5.2	**SOP*** Required	**Records Required?**** Yes
Summary of Requirements		
The organization must take corrective action to eliminate causes, and prevent recurrence, of nonconformities. Corrective action must be appropriate to impact of problems encountered. Documented procedure for corrective action must define requirements for: • Identifying nonconformities (including customer complaints). • Determining causes of nonconformity. • Evaluating need for actions to ensure that nonconformities do not recur. • Determining and implementing corrective action needed. • Recording results of action taken. • Reviewing of corrective action taken.		
*Question 18. **Question 22.		

ISO 9004: 2000 Guidelines—Performance Improvement
Title   Corrective action
Clause 8.5.2
Summary of Guidelines

Plan and establish a process for corrective action. Planning should include evaluation of significance of problems affecting quality. Evaluation should study potential impact on such aspects as:
• Costs of nonconformance.
• Customer satisfaction.
• Dependability.
• Operating costs.
• Performance.
• Safety.

As input for corrective action, use:
• Customer complaints.
• Internal audit reports.
• Nonconformance reports.
• Outputs from management review.
• Outputs from data analysis.
• Outputs from satisfaction measurements.
• Process measurements.
• Relevant QMS records.
• Results of self-assessment.

Involve appropriate functions in corrective action process. Focus corrective action on eliminating causes of nonconformances and defects so as to avoid recurrence. As part of in the corrective process:
• Identify sources of information.
• Collect information.
• Define causes of nonconformances and defects.
• Verify root cause analysis results by testing, where appropriate.
• Eliminate causes of nonconformances and defects.
• Take appropriate actions to avoid recurrence of problems.
• Keep records of activity and results.

When corrective actions are taken, emphasize efficiency and process effectiveness. Monitor corrective actions to ensure that desired goals are met.

Include corrective actions in management review process, especially corrective actions with:
• High financial impact.
• Significant potential impact on customer satisfaction.

Transition Guidance: ISO 9001: 1994 to ISO 9001: 2000	
ISO 9001: 1994 Cross-Reference	4.14.1 Corrective action
Summary of Differences	Essentially the same. More specific as to purpose of corrective action—to prevent "recurrence" of non-conformities. Only potential substantive difference is requirement for review of corrective action taken (this would seem to replace the "effectiveness" requirement in 1994).
Quality Policy Manual Updates	Add language addressing review of corrective action.
Procedure Updates	Update system and procedure to reflect review of corrective action.
See Question	100

73. What is preventive action all about?

CAPSULE ANSWER

The preventive action process heads off a potential nonconformity by identifying its cause(s) and implementing solutions *before* the nonconformity actually occurs.

Unlike corrective action (Question 72), preventive action is a process for identifying *potential* problems—nonconformities that have not occurred yet—and taking action to *prevent* them from happening.

PITFALL

Of the changes made to the Standard in the 1994 revision, "preventive action" was probably the least implemented by organizations.

You are required to develop and implement a system for identifying such potential problems, determining potential causes, implementing preventive actions to keep nonconformities from occurring, and checking back to make sure that the preventive action was effective.

This is proactive quality management, and a whole new level for firms accustomed to the more reactive, fire-fighting approach. To believe in this, you have to believe that an ounce of prevention is worth a pound of cure. Leading edge organizations that have truly implemented preventive action have found it to be a very powerful tool—but to make it work requires re-education of the workforce and a whole new mindset.

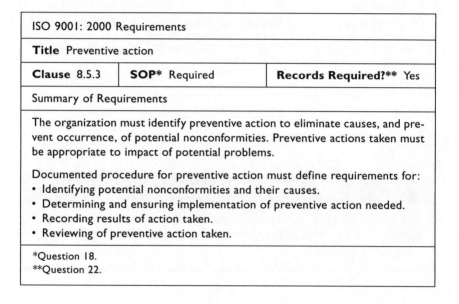

ISO 9001: 2000 Requirements		
Title Preventive action		
Clause 8.5.3	**SOP*** Required	**Records Required?**** Yes
Summary of Requirements		
The organization must identify preventive action to eliminate causes, and prevent occurrence, of potential nonconformities. Preventive actions taken must be appropriate to impact of potential problems. Documented procedure for preventive action must define requirements for: • Identifying potential nonconformities and their causes. • Determining and ensuring implementation of preventive action needed. • Recording results of action taken. • Reviewing of preventive action taken.		
*Question 18. **Question 22.		

ISO 9004: 2000 Guidelines—Performance Improvement
Title   Preventive action
Clause 8.5.3
Summary of Guidelines
To identify causes of potential nonconformances, use preventive methodologies including: • Criticality analyses. • Failure modes and effects. • Fault tree analysis. • Risk analyses.

(Continued)

- Statistical process control.
- Trend analyses.

Involve appropriate organizational representatives in preventive actions.

In planning and prioritizing preventive actions, identify sources of information, including:
- Customer needs and expectations.
- Management review output.
- Market analysis.
- Outputs from data analysis.
- Process measurements.
- Processes that provide early warning of approaching out-of-control operating conditions.
- Relevant QMS records.
- Results of self-assessment.
- Satisfaction measurements.
- Systems that consolidate many sources of customer information.

Include preventive actions in management review, especially preventive actions with:
- High financial impact.
- Significant potential impact on satisfaction of customers and other interested parties.

Transition Guidance: ISO 9001: 1994 to ISO 9001: 2000	
ISO 9001: 1994 Cross-Reference	4.14.3 Preventive action
Summary of Differences	More specific as to purpose of preventive action—to prevent "occurrence" of potential nonconformities. Requirement for review of preventive action is new also.
Quality Policy Manual Updates	Update to include more specific purpose, as well as review requirement.
Procedure Updates	Add preventive action review to system and procedure.
See Question	100

PART THREE

Implementing—A First-Timer's Guide

There are two ways to implement an ISO 9000 system. You can go the slap-dash route. Knock out some documents, teach people the buzz terms, hew closely to "the way we've always done things," and make only the changes that you must absolutely make to just barely meet the requirements of the Standard. And then find the easiest, tamest registrar you can, and pray that you "pass."

That costs money.

Or, you can go the more thoughtful route. Rather than treating ISO 9000 implementation as a get-it-over-with race, treat it as an opportunity not only to improve how your organization runs, but also to set the stage for ongoing improvement into the future.

That costs money, too. But it's also the route that *pays.*

The more cynical among us (organizations and consultants alike) think of ISO 9000 as a paperwork thing, a formality, an add-on. The more progressive—and, I submit, the true leaders—think of it as a platform, a structure, a mechanism by which management can guide the organization toward ever increasing efficiencies at meeting customer needs and minimizing costs.

Whichever route you choose, the guidance in this section will help you. It is based on the results of dozens of implementations in organizations of all kinds—all distilled into what we like to think of as rather generic and immutable principles. Every organization and every implementation is different. One size definitely does not fit all.

But here are some strategies you'll find useful in making your own implementation journey.

74. How should we plan and schedule our implementation program?

CAPSULE ANSWER

There are four generic phases to ISO 9000 implementation and a logical order to the steps.

Every implementation is different. Even within industries, organizations differ widely, and implementing ISO 9000 is, to an extent, a custom-designed effort.

PITFALL

If there was ever an initiative where good project planning is needed, ISO 9000 implementation is it. Yet some organizations flounder for lack of effective planning.

Even so, there is a set of fairly standard "phases" through which each implementation proceeds. There is a logical order to the process. Some of this is intuitively obvious. Some of it has been learned through experience.

These phases are not necessarily discrete. They can overlap quite a bit. The phases will not necessarily fit the exact timetables you estimate for them, either. A certain amount of "winging it" is to be expected here.

PHASE 1: PREPARATION

Management Commitment

Why does this come first? Because without it you might as well not invest another nickel's worth of time or resources on the process. Senior management must commit itself, at the outset, to the process. It must also stay involved as the process moves forward.

Planning, Scheduling, Staffing, Budgeting

Plot out your schedule on a spreadsheet. It should have at least 12 columns. Each represents one month. Most organizations start with a date by which they must be registered. In some cases, this is prescribed by customers. Find out if customers have deadlines for registration. If no customer is imposing a deadline at this time, you can set your own target.

Write your target month for registration in the last column on your spreadsheet. Then back up a minimum of 4 months from that—and preferably 6 months. That month is called "D-Day." It is the month by which your ISO 9000 systems must be designed, in place, and operating. They do not have to be fully functional, debugged, "perfect." (No system is ever "perfect," not even years down the road.) But it should be in place and running a minimum of 3, and preferably 6, months before registration audit. This is so there is sufficient evidence and records to prove that the system is in place.

Now back up 6 months from D-Day. On average, this is the month you must start the implementation process in order to have enough time to get the job done. So what we are looking at, on average, is about one year to implement the system, from start to finish.

If the month you've picked for your start date is already two or three months in the past, then you'll have to do one of two things:

1. Compress your schedule so that you meet the required deadline.
2. Extend your deadline.

Now the project needs to be staffed. Senior management must appoint a Management Representative (MR) (Question 30) to lead the effort. The MR should have a deputy, as well as dedicated staff support. Other functions need to be drawn into the process now, too, including members for a Quality Steering Team (QST) (Question 30).

As for budgeting, at this point you can plug numbers for the following. (Question 8 has more information on implementation costs.)

■ Overview training—30 minutes of time for every employee in the organization.
■ Orientation training—perhaps 90 minutes of time for every employee in the organization. (This is a hard one to call.)

■ Internal audit training—Two days of time for a number of employees equal to about 10 percent of your head count.

■ Internal audit costs (this one is very iffy)—an average of 4 hours per audit for 2 auditors (total of 8 hours per audit), times the number of standard operating procedures in your system (at least 20, could be as many as 26). Remember that at least one complete cycle of internal audits must be completed before registration audit.

■ Equipment, supplies, and so on, including a good computer with word processing software and the services of someone who knows how to use it.

■ Registrar services—see Question 93 for details.

Project Launch

PITFALL

It is important to have a plan. But one thing about ISO 9000 implementation is that you have to run your organization, too—you can't just shut down to "do ISO." For that reason, as in war, the first casualty of the process is often the plan.

This begins by getting ISO 9000 orientation training for senior management. This must include the CEO, the general manager, or whoever is in charge of the organization. It must also include the Quality Steering Team (QST). Normally this can be done in a day or less, but *it must be done*.

Next, senior management needs to create the organization's Quality Policy Statement (Question 26). This may take some time. It is subject to change, of course. But senior management should put sincere effort into making the statement:

■ Relevant to the needs and expectations of customers.
■ Specific to the organization.

Senior management then announces the process to the organization, along with the plan and schedule. At this point the response of the employees will most likely be a collective "HUH?" That is all right. They will be taken care of in subsequent phases.

PHASE 2: DOCUMENTATION

The process for creating the quality system documents is discussed in Questions 80–83.

- Create the initial Standard Operating Procedures (Question 18). These are needed to facilitate the creation and issue of the other documents in the system.
- Create the balance of the Standard Operating Procedures.
- Create, approve, and issue the Quality Policy Manual (Question 20).
- Create the necessary work instructions.

PHASE 3: TRAINING

PITFALL

Make sure people get *just* the training they need. They are not responsible for knowing about parts of the ISO 9000 system that are not relevant to their job functions.

Two types of training are involved here. The first type is training in the internal audit function. The other type of training is awareness and orientation training. It is very important that this is done on a planned, phased basis. The worst mistake you can make is to hurl the ISO 9000 system at your people at the last minute!

See Question 79 for details on training.

PHASE 4: CRUNCH TIME

This is the period between D-Day—when all elements of the system have been set up and are functioning—and registration audit time. Think of it as a "shake-down cruise" for your ISO 9000 system. Think of it also as white knuckle time. Time is the issue; you will feel that there just isn't enough time to get everything squared away and running properly.

It is during "crunch time" that the skeptics of the organization have their day. To them, nothing is working right. It is limping along. It'll never work, never pay off. There are all of these new dumb ISO rules "keeping us from doing our jobs." Let them vent. It does them good. Just stay the course.

During crunch time, all employees should be "working the system." This means that they are:

- Aware of the procedures that affect how they do their jobs.
- Working in a way that is consistent with those procedures.
- Requesting changes to documents where they feel they are needed.
- Reporting quality related problems via the Corrective and Preventive Action system (including whatever "dumb things" about the ISO 9000 process that crop up).
- Dealing with and resolving quality-related problems via the Corrective and Preventive Action system.

Other activities during crunch time include:

- *Management reviews.* Although, once your system is established, it is all right to hold perhaps 2 or 3 of these per year, during implementation you should hold a formal management review at least once a month. This keeps senior management tightly focused on the progress of the implementation. It also keeps them from having any surprises.
- *Orientation training* (Question 79) continues. It should be wrapped up early during this period.

OPPORTUNITY

Internal auditing gives employees a chance to learn more about the organization's processes, in parts of the organization with which they may not be familiar.

- *Internal audits.* This is the most important activity during crunch time. The audits tend to drive the process.
  — They get people really focused on what the documents say.
  — They provide essential information to senior management on how the process is going.

— They give employees some real-world experience in being audited—experience that will stand them in good stead when registration audit time comes.

— Audits are in fact a very fine teaching tool.

■ *Select and schedule registration body.* This process should begin prior to D-day and be concluded shortly thereafter (Question 93).

PHASE 5: THE "LAST" LAP

Suddenly the system starts to take hold. People begin to understand it and get comfortable with it. After your first cycle of internal audits passes, and deficiencies arising from the audits are taken care of, the system fits a lot better. Now the workforce starts to feel that maybe this ISO thing is not so bad after all.

During the "last lap" (which is actually, to use Winston Churchill's phrase, not the beginning of the end, but the end of the beginning), the following activities take place:

■ *Pre-Assessment (Readiness Review).* This gives you a final shot at fine-tuning your system before registration audit (Question 94).

■ *Registration assessment.* The big day!

OPPORTUNITY

During pre-assessment (not required but highly recommended), have the auditors check the parts of the system *that you are most uncertain about.*

75. Internally, who should we involve in the implementation process from the start?

CAPSULE ANSWER

Implementation begins with the senior manager and fans out to involve the operational and line managers as time goes on.

Implementing ISO 9000 effectively is, clearly, a top-down process. Commitment and involvement starts at the top, and then spreads out gradually over the weeks and months.

The *first* person involved must be the *senior manager* of the organization—the CEO or general manager. This does not mean that he or she actively runs the implementation process, in most organizations, even very small ones. (This would, however, not be a bad idea.) But the senior manager gives the green light, gets the ball rolling, provides resources, solves disputes, and maintains oversight to make sure the process continues to move along (Question 87).

PITFALL

The Quality Steering Team must include key people from *every* part of the process(es).

Next is a group called the *Quality Steering Team*. This is made up of the senior manager, plus the managers of each functional element of the organization, as appropriate:

- Administration.
- Data processing.
- Design.
- Finance/accounting.
- Manufacturing.
- Research and development.
- Sales and marketing.
- Service.
- Shipping and warehouse.
- Training/human resources.

This group is actively responsible for carrying out the approved implementation plan. It is trained in ISO 9000 principles almost at the beginning of the project (Question 79). Its activities should be documented in a standard operating procedure, and records should be kept of its actions. It meets regularly (no less often than once per month, between launch and registration). Generally, its responsibilities include:

- Monitoring progress on the implementation plan, and making adjustments as needed.
- Reviewing and approving policy documents and standard operating procedures.
- Approving proposed solutions to gaps in compliance (especially where these crossover functional lines).
- Resolving operational disputes among departments and functions.
- Reviewing and approving corrective and preventive actions.
- Reviewing registrar proposals and selecting the registrar.

The top functional manager in each area need not attend every single meeting. Much of this work can be (and usually is) delegated. But the top functional managers should be actively involved in the process. Otherwise, their subordinates get the wrong message.

The Quality Steering Team often remains a permanent body after the implementation is complete. At the very least, its members usually comprise the group that carries out Management Review (Question 31).

The "first among equals" in the Quality Steering Team is the *Management Representative.* This is the person responsible to the senior manager for effective implementation and maintenance of the quality system (Question 30).

As the implementation proceeds, the next to be brought on board are the line managers, foremen, supervisors, and leaders. (In very small organizations, these may in fact be the "senior managers" who sit on the Quality Steering Team.) Usually, their involvement begins with overview training and then gets more intense as they start to review the quality system documents during the documentation phase.

Historically, this group is the most difficult to motivate. Of everyone, they are the most involved and focused on short-term, deadline-related, production-oriented issues. They have little time for "theory" (to use a polite term), and often resent senior management for "inflicting" ISO 9000 on them.

The question is often raised: "What's the easiest way to get middle management on board?" There is no "easiest" way. There is in fact no easy way at all. Though some embrace the process at once, others won't see anything like a direct benefit for a long time. To them, it will seem only like a lot of wasted time and useless paperwork. The best tactic here seems to be an enlightened mix of carrot and stick. The "carrot" is senior management's professed confidence that the ISO 9000 process will help improve organization performance, thereby benefiting all. The "stick" is that we are all in deep trouble if we do not get this done!

76. In what sequence should we develop and implement our quality management system?

CAPSULE ANSWER

In general, successful implementations follow a logical, "additive" sequence.

ISO 9001: 2000 is structured more or less in process order. So the way it is laid out makes intuitive sense. It is not, however, set up in implementation order.

What follows in this section is a layout of a generic implementation sequence, a sort of blueprint. It has been developed, modified, and proven over many dozens of implementations, in organizations of all sizes and process descriptions.

This sequence is not etched in stone, by any means. Some variation is to be expected, depending on the unique circumstances of your organization. But the general pattern assures a relatively smooth process and a relative lack of "do-over."

Note: A great deal of the work is in the area of documentation. Whether procedures are required, recommended, or not needed is addressed in Question 18. This information is also provided with the question relating to each requirement. Develop the needed documentation as you work each phase, following the guidance in Questions 80–83.

Phase/Notes	Description	Question	Clause
Implementation Team Identify and appoint management rep and quality steering team	Management representative	30	5.5.3
Document System • Determine format for procedures and instructions	General documentation requirements	18	4.2
• Determine control system	QMS Internal communication	19	5.5.4
	Control of documents	21	5.5.6
Records Control • Set system for identifying required records as implementation proceeds • As records are identified, specify retention intervals • Determine methods for control • Document and implement process	Control of records	22	5.5.7
Improvement • Develop and implement corrective/preventive action procedures • Implement	Corrective action	72	8.5.2
	Preventive action	73	8.5.3
Top Management • Set management review procedure and schedule	Management review	31	5.6
• Set QMS policies and objectives • Determine method for publicizing, enforcing, updating these	Management responsibility— General requirements	23	5.1
• Identify methods for determining customer requirements and assuring that they are understood throughout organization	Customer focus	24	5.2
	Legal requirements	25	None
• Document responsibility/ authority structure	Quality policy	26	5.3
• Determine resource requirements	Quality objectives	27	5.4.1
• Assure that needed resources are available	Quality planning	28	5.4.2

(continued)

(Continued)

Phase/Notes	Description	Question	Clause
	QMS Responsibility and authority	29	5.5.2
	Resource management	32	6.1
	Resources—Information	35	None
	Resources—Facilities	36	6.3
	Resources—Work environment	36	6.4
Training • Document qualifications and skills of personnel • Develop and document hiring/training system • Implement	Assignment of personnel	33	6.2.1
	Training, awareness, competency	34	6.2.2
Product/Service Design • Are you design responsible? (If not, see "scope reduction") • Update design process to bring into compliance • Document design process • Implement design process	Design and development—General	43	7.3.1
	Design input	44	7.3.2
	Design output	45	7.3.3
	Design review	46	7.3.4
	Design verification	47	7.3.5
	Design validation	48	7.3.6
	Control of changes	49	7.3.7
Customer Communication • Determine system for customer requirements: identifying, reviewing, communicating • Determine system for customer communication • Document and implement	ID of customer requirements	52	7.2.1
	Review of customer requirements	53	7.2.2
	Customer communication	51	7.2.3

(Continued)

Phase/Notes	Description	Question	Clause
Creating Product/Service • Ensure that all applicable requirements are met • Identify and document non-relevant requirements for "scope reduction"	Product and/or service realization: general requirements	50	7.1
Purchasing • Develop and document vendor selection process • Develop and document purchasing process • Develop and document method(s) for verifying purchased product/service • Implement	Purchasing control	54	7.4.1
	Purchasing information	55	7.4.2
	Verification of purchased product	56	7.4.3
Control of Processes • Determine and document production process(es) through delivery/provision to customer • Determine and document verification process(es) • Determine and document methods for controlling nonconformity • Identify processes requiring validation • Where applicable, determine and document validation methods (where not applicable, exclude via scope reduction) • Determine customer property and control thereof (where not applicable, exclude via scope reduction) • Implement	Operations control	57	7.5.1
	Customer property	60	7.5.3
	ID and traceability	59	7.5.2
	Measurement—Product	58	8.2.4
	Control of nonconformity	69	8.3
	Validation of processes	40	7.5.5
	Preservation of product	58	7.5.4
Calibration • Identify devices requiring control • Determine and document control methods • Implement	Control of measurement and monitoring devices	62	7.6

(continued)

(Continued)

Phase/Notes	Description	Question	Clause
Process Design and Improvement • Determine system for design and update of processes • Determine methods for improving processes • Document and implement	Design of processes	39	None
	Measurement/ monitoring of processes	41	8.2.3
	Improvement of processes	42	None
Internal Audit • Develop internal audit process • Appoint and train auditors • Document and implement	Internal audit	68	8.2.2
Measurement, Analysis, Improvement • Determine methods for measurement and analysis • Determine methods for measuring satisfaction of customers and other groups • Document and implement	Measurement, analysis, and improvement	63	None
	Improvement— General	71	8.5.1
	Measurement/ analysis: general	64	8.1
	Measurement— Customer satisfaction	65	8.2.1
	Measurement satisfaction other groups	66	None
	Analysis of data	70	8.4
	Business finance, self assessment	67	None
Scope Reduction Identify and list elements from Section 7 that are not relevant to process/system	Permissible exclusions	14	1.2
Quality Policy Manual Document quality policies in manual	QMS quality manual	20	5.5.5

77. When organizations start working on ISO 9000, what elements of the Standard are most often found to be lacking?

Capsule Answer

Though most well-run organizations already meet many of the requirements to an extent, there is a set of requirements that virtually *no* organization meets at the outset.

This may be hard to believe, but it is true: The typical organization already meets the majority of ISO 9000 requirements. At least in *some* sense. The problem they encounter is twofold:

1. The organization's systems may not be documented/recorded as required by the ISO 9000 Standard.
2. The system is often not thoroughly implemented or consistently followed.

As an example: The Standard requires that contracts (customer orders) be reviewed to ensure that:

- All required information (customer requirements) is present and accurate.
- The organization has the ability to meet customer requirements.

Every organization already does this. It has to. So, technically, every organization is in compliance with this requirement. But the means by which the organization does this is, typically, not formalized. Often, the required amount of record-keeping is not present, either. Different employees are doing the tasks in slightly different ways.

Pitfall

Do not assume that this list is comprehensive or universal. Every organization is different. Some lack processes that one would normally expect—like calibration. It is not a bad idea to have a professional do an initial assessment of your system and give you a listing of your compliance "gaps."

In large part, the process of implementing an ISO 9000 system is a matter of formalizing and documenting what is already being done. This has the natural effect of making things more consistent, too, since everyone whose work is affected by a procedure is required to work in accordance with the procedure.

But in the real world, the typical organization, lacks at the outset compliance to several key elements. The number and identity of these elements depends upon the extent to which the organization has implemented Total Quality Management or other quality-related disciplines in the past. Here are the requirements that are almost never met by the typical organization getting involved in ISO 9000:

Clause	Description	Question
5.4	Policy—Understood, implemented, and current	26
5.5.1	Planning—Quality objectives: defined and documented	27
5.5.2	Planning—Quality planning: formalized	28
5.6.3	Management representative—"champion" for the quality process (note: needs *not* be a "quality manager" or a full time position)	30
5.6.6	Control of documents—System to ensure use only of current approved quality related documents	21
5.6.7	Control of records—Formalized process for storage, retention times, and so on	22
5.7	Management review—Regular top level process to review status and effectiveness of the QMS	31
7.5.3	Customer property—System for ensuring its protection and control	60
7.5.5	Validation of processes of whose output the quality cannot be independently judged	40
8.2.1.1	Measurement—Customer satisfaction: objective and formalized system	64
8.2.1.2	Internal audit —Regular formalized and documented audits of status of QMS	68
8.4	Analysis of data for improvement—Applying "lessons learned" to improvement of processes	70
8.5.2	Corrective action—Disciplined, formalized system for eliminating causes of quality related problems	72
8.5.3	Preventive action—Disciplined, formalized system for eliminating causes of potential quality related problems	73
8.5.4	Improvement of processes—Formalized methodology	42

78. If our organization has more than one location, what is the best way to set up our quality system?

CAPSULE ANSWER

The way you structure your quality system in a multiple-location company depends in large part on the activities carried out at each location.

There are a couple of different ways to go. You need to decide what is best for your organization.

First, establish what is actually done at each location. There are two types of locations.

1. A site is a location that has a production process and makes things. Typically, it must always be assessed and registered to ISO 9000 if its customers are requiring it to register.
2. A remote location is one that does not produce things. Usually, remote locations carry out activities like these:
   — Accounting
   — Administration
   — Engineering
   — Purchasing
   — Sales
   — Warehousing

A remote location cannot be registered to ISO 9000 on its own. But each remote location that supports a site (see above) must:

■ Undergo registration assessment.
■ Be included in that site's ISO 9000 registration.

Certain types of remote locations (not all of them) may be audited on a "sampling" basis during registration and/or surveillance assessments. The number of such sites sampled and the amount of time devoted to each is at the discretion of the registration body. The rule of thumb is that such locations can be sampled as long as they do not add value to the dimensions or attributes of the product or service that the organization provides. Obvious candidates here are sales or distribution locations.

Having said all that, what are the options for your multiple site
organization?

- You can register each site, with the remote locations that support
  it, separately. You must do this if:
  — The sites have separate and distinguishable quality systems. If
    each has its own quality manual (Question 20), then the sites
    have separate quality systems.
  — The sites each ship separately, and independently, to cus-
    tomers, and never (or virtually never) ship parts or compo-
    nents to each other. This means you have totally separate
    processes, which virtually mandates separate quality systems.
- You can obtain a corporate scheme registration, if your registra-
  tion body offers this. With this, all locations (sites and their remote locations) are assessed and then registered under a single
  certificate.
  — You may do this if all sites work to a single quality system (i.e.,
    common quality manual), that is centrally managed. This
    means a single quality manual, and a management representa-
    tive that oversees the quality system at all locations. Lower tier
    documentation may vary from site to site, and you could also
    have local "quality representatives" running things on a day to
    day basis. But the overall system must cover all locations.
  — This approach is optimal when the sites and locations are
    within a reasonable geographical distance of each other.

It may be in your long-term business interest to obtain a corporate
scheme registration, if your organization is eligible. Here is why:

- It could end up costing you less money. The audit days requirements per site (Question 93) can be less than for individual site
  registration. This means you may pay less for the registration audit

and for surveillance audits. Only a careful evaluation of quotes from several registrars can confirm this.

■ If your locations interact a great deal, placing them all under a common, centrally managed quality system could improve communication, quality, and results. On the other hand, if your locations operate autonomously now from a quality/management standpoint, placing them under a common quality system could be a wrenching experience and could add to the stress and strain of doing the implementation. It takes an exceptionally strong and determined senior management team to make the project fly, under these circumstances.

As a practical matter, you should confer with at least one registration body on your "corporate scheme" before proceeding with implementation. They can look at your structure and your system, tell you about your options, and provide cost figures.

79. What types of training should we provide to employees during the implementation process?

CAPSULE ANSWER

You must provide all employees with QMS orientation and awareness training on a phased, easy-to-understand basis. You must also train your internal audit team.

Training is a big part of successful implementation. Even if your employees have been involved in TQM or related quality practices before, many aspects of ISO 9000 will be new to them.

Two types of training are discussed here. One is training for internal auditors—critical to the success of your implementation and of the QMS in general.

The other type of training is ISO 9000 orientation and awareness training. This is where many organizations drop the ball. This type of training must be provided on a phased basis—a little at a time, over a period of time, in reasonable, easy-to-digest chunks. The exact wrong approach is to call everyone into a room, dump a pile of manuals in their laps, order them to "learn all this by Friday, we're getting audited."

Awareness Training

This is a very rudimentary overview session. It can be done in very large groups. It should be:

- Carried out within days of project launch.
- Thirty minutes (or less) in length.
- Motivating as well as educational.
- Reassuring (your whole world is not going to change).

OPPORTUNITY

The organization president can send a powerful message by attending and participating in the internal audit training.

The session should give all employees a snapshot of:

- What ISO 9000 is.
- Why your organization is getting involved.
- How the system will affect them.

Orientation Training

This trains employees in the key facts about the ISO 9000 system that *every employee must know*. The critical issues on this training are:

- It should be done about a month after the awareness training, but no more than 90 days afterward.

OPPORTUNITY

Support the training with creative strategies such as posters, impromptu quizzes, reminder stuffers in employee paychecks.

- It should be conducted by the employees' direct supervisors, not by HR or training personnel. They have to get knowledgeable enough about the ISO 9000 process in order to do the training.
- It should take no more than one hour to complete.

The training should address the Five Key Facts:

1. The name of your quality system (ISO 9001).
2. Knowledge of the quality policy statement.
3. Location of quality system documents that affect employees.
4. The system for requesting changes to quality system documents. ("We need your help in getting these documents right, and keeping them up to date.")
5. The system for reporting quality-related problems for action (Corrective and Preventive Action system). ("You know what the quality problems are. We need your help addressing them.")

The training should also address upcoming activities:

- Internal audits.
- Registration audits.
- Surveillance audits.

OPPORTUNITY

One organization, as it got close to registration audit, quizzed employees on the 5 key facts—while handing out paychecks!

Prepare a brief quiz consisting of maybe 10 or 12 questions on the above facts. Have the employees complete the quiz on an open-book basis. They can even work on it in pairs, if they want to. Go over the answers and then have them turn the quiz in.

INTERNAL AUDIT TRAINING

This is mandatory training for the team you select as internal auditors (Question 68). Scheduling is critical here: The training needs to take place right around the time the first wave of operational Standard

Operating Procedures are ready to implement. This allows you to set the audit schedule and start auditing promptly upon completion of the training which maximizes the effectiveness of the training.

Normally, the course runs for two days. A good course will address the following:

- ISO 9000 requirements.
- Purpose of auditing.
- Strategic importance of auditing.
- The phases of a typical audit.
- Audit planning.
- Gathering of data.
- Importance of evidence.
- Rationalizing findings.
- Documenting and reporting findings.
- Audit follow-up.
- Human relations issues surrounding the audit process.

It is not a bad idea to train a very large group to be internal auditors. This gives you back-up in case certain individuals drop out, either because they find they do not care for the activity, or because they change assignments.

FUNCTIONAL TRAINING

This is a second session of department training, carried out by department supervisors. It should be carried out during the period surrounding D-Day and must be done no later than 30 days before your registration pre-assessment. Each session will run perhaps 60 to 90 minutes. The topics of this training are:

- Repeat of the Five Key Facts taught in the Orientation Training (above).
- Review of the procedures, work instructions, and other documents that the employees are responsible for following.

Your employees will find problems, flaws, and so on in the procedures and work instructions. This is to be expected. It is highly desirable! Be sure to have them initiate Corrective Action Requests so that the problems they find are addressed and fixed.

Finish the session by giving the employees the same quiz you gave them at the end of the orientation training. This time, however, it is a closed-book quiz. Go over the answers with them at the end.

80. What are the rules for creating effective quality system documents?

CAPSULE ANSWER

By following the ten commandments, you will have a document system that is lean, easy to understand, and useful to the employees who are required to comply with it.

The Standard does not prescribe any such rules. This is left strictly up to you. Long experience with implementing ISO 9000 systems has, however, taught that good, effective, easy to use document systems have certain common characteristics.

After all, these are not documents to be stuck in a notebook and thrust on some high shelf somewhere. These are not documents reserved for the sole use of managers and auditors. These are not documents that contain state secrets. These documents describe and specify how the quality system works. They spell out the approved methods for operating the processes (including, sometimes, tasks within the processes). They define the methods used to assure that the results of the process meet customer and/or internal requirements.

We want the documents to be clear, specific (to an extent), and easy to read and to use. What's the appropriate reading level? Sixth to eighth grade at the absolute highest. What about our people who don't read at that level? Create even simpler documents for them. What about non-English-speaking employees? Get them translations. Everyone must be included. (But you need only translate the documents *directly relevant* to the jobs of the people using them.)

Here, then, are the field-tested, highly unofficial, and virtually immutable ten commandments:

1. *Make each document prove that it must exist.* Often, you will be adapting existing documents for use in your system. But the mere fact that a document exists today does not mean that it must exist and be

PITFALL

You're not being paid by the word and masses of documents impress no auditors. Keep your system lean.

included in your ISO 9000 system. No document has an intrinsic right to exist. Perhaps a week, a month, a decade ago someone thought the document was a good idea. It may not be a good idea now. You need to make a judgment on this—with every single document. So take a zero-based approach to existing documents.

2. *Make each document consistent and compatible with other documents in the system.* This is a must. Look at the Document Hierarchy in Question 18.

- The quality manual must be consistent with the ISO 9000 standard (and must address all the "shalls" in the standard).
- The Standard Operating Procedures must be consistent and compatible with the Quality Manual.
- The work instructions must be consistent and compatible with the Standard Operating Procedures.

This means that the people doing the writing must have access to all the documents in the system. They must make it a practice to review related documents to ensure consistency and compatibility among them.

3. *Where possible, structure documents in the sequence of the activities you are documenting.* This is just common sense. People understand things better when they are expressed in process order. This even applies to the quality policy manual (Question 20). If you structure it the way the ISO 9001: 2000 standard is structured, it too will follow process order (more or less).

OPPORTUNITY

There is nothing wrong with incorporating graphics, such as flow charts and diagrams, with your procedures, if by doing so you improve usability. Work instructions are often created in pictorial form.

But SOPs and work instructions are another matter. These tend to have a sequence to them, since they describe how processes are carried out. It only makes sense to structure them in sequence. You would be surprised how often this does not happen. Documents written out of sequence cause unending problems for users (and, for what difference it makes, for auditors, too).

4. *Where document text varies with actual practice, initiate a corrective action request so that the practice is reviewed and changed.* As SOPs and work instructions are written, it is often decided to change the actual practices. This tends to be done for two reasons:

    a. The existing practice does not comply with the Standard, and has to be changed.

    b. Management decides to change the practice to improve quality, efficiency, consistency, and so on.

Great. But just because you write down a different practice does not mean that people will respond the way you want them to. To make sure that the practices themselves change, write a Corrective Action Request citing the old practice and recommending the new practice, and assign it to the responsible manager in accordance with the system outlined in your SOP for Corrective Action. This way, the change doesn't fall through a crack.

5. *Make documents operationally tolerant.* Too often, managers view the document writing process as a chance to tighten things up. They want to get super-specific and prescriptive about every single step. This is a mistake. Such tactics not only alienate employees, they also result in documents that are lengthy, bloated, difficult to read, and (ultimately) ignored.

When writing SOPs and work instructions, keep in mind the qualifications of the functions that are carrying out the activities. (These qualifications are written down and you would do well to review them during the writing.) Then write the documents so that they are only specific enough to assure that the requirements—the "musts"—of the process are covered, and that the result of the process will meet customer and/or internal requirements. Rely on the experience, training, and good judgment of the employees to take care of the rest.

6. *Use functional titles, not personal names.* Remember that these documents must keep up with the times. They must be accurate always. But people come and go. Employees transfer, change jobs, and so on. When you use personal names in the documents, then the documents have to be revised, updated, and re-issued each time an individual changes jobs. This results in unnecessary paperwork.

So use functional titles instead. It is rather impersonal and non-people-oriented, which is unfortunate. But it saves a lot of work and headaches.

7. *Use present tense only.* These documents describe how activities are carried out now. They do not describe how activities will be carried out in the future. Some document writers adopt a prescriptive, lawyerly sentence structure that uses "future tense" as if they were writing statutes or laws. We want to write what is happening now. Therefore, instead of saying:

> *The Sales Manager will sign each contract after review.*

Say this:

> *The Sales Manager signs each contract after review.*

This means the words and expressions like "will," "shall," "is to be," and so on are banned. Eliminating these words has the additional merit of making sentences shorter.

PITFALL

Make the documents speak the users' language, or they will never embrace them.

---

8. *Make documents pithy: short words, sentences, paragraphs.* Writing short is probably the single most important attribute of effective quality system documents.

- Strive always to find the clearest, most direct, and shortest way of saying things.
- Use every day words. SOPs and work instructions are not chances for you to show off your $500 vocabulary.
- Keep sentences short. An average of nine words or less is highly desirable. Ban use of the semicolon (;). It has no place in these documents.
- Keep paragraphs skinny. Big blocks of type are hard to read. Use bullets and outlining styles, too.

■ Documents tend to find their own length. You can write short all you want, and you may still end up with documents that motor on for a few pages. In cases like this, try to break the documents up. An SOP that is longer than 3 to 4 pages is likely to be an SOP that is not read. Ditto for work instructions.

9. *Explain acronyms when first used.* Every organization has its own jargon. In many firms, the jargon is acronyms. Some firms are more acronym-happy than others. In some, entire conversations can be conducted in acronyms ("I did ACDUTRA at CNAVRES"). There is nothing wrong with that, except for the poor slob who has to figure out what these clumps of capitals mean when sorting through the quality manual, SOPs, and work instructions.

You may think that "everyone" knows what these things mean, but rest assured, "everyone" does not. New employees don't, and they will be reading these documents. Neither do people from other areas of your organization, necessarily. Finally, there are the external (registration) auditors to think about. The better they understand your system, the smoother your audit will go. Count on it.

So, in each document, explain each acronym with the first usage, as in "Standard Operating Procedure (SOP)." Afterward, use the acronym only.

10. *When in doubt, leave it out.* One of your main tasks will be to keep your entire system as lean as possible. The only way to do this is to be even more vigilant about leaving things out than you are about putting things in.

81. Instead of creating procedures and other documents from scratch, can we adapt documents we already have?

CAPSULE ANSWER

Adapting existing documents can be a good shortcut to doing the document writing job—but there are pitfalls.

Certainly. This is, in fact, a common approach where an organization similar to yours already has a quality manual, you can use that as a starting point to create yours. You may already have documents within your organization that can be adapted to serve as procedures, work instructions, and forms.

Adapting existing documents can save time and effort. But this approach is not a quick fix, and there are dangers involved, if you are not careful:

- It is unwise to simply lift existing procedures and work instructions and throw them into your ISO 9000 system without thorough review. Just because you have procedures and work instructions in your organization already, that does not mean that they are right. It also does not mean that people are actually following them.
- It is risky to take someone else's procedures (or quality manual, for that matter), put your name on them, and put them into practice without thorough review. You may think the organization from which you acquired the documents is "exactly like" yours, but, rest assured, it is not. No two organizations are exactly the same.
- When organizations adapt existing documents, they sometimes gloss over the text without fully understanding what it says. This can cause them to say things they do not really mean. This often happens with the quality manual. There is a tendency to treat the quality manual as "boilerplate" and simply knock it out without understanding what the words really mean.
- Organizations that adapt their own (or someone else's) document systems also run the risk of having systems that are too large, too complicated, too unwieldy. The mere fact that a document exists today does not mean it is worth having and using tomorrow.

To adapt existing documents for your ISO 9000 system, do the following:

- Before doing any writing or adapting, define the format and structure for each type of quality system document. (This is a one-time exercise.) Each section of the quality manual should be structured the same way, with common headings, and so on. Similarly, define a standard format and structure for procedures and work instructions to follow.
- *Step 1: Decide if the document really has to exist.* Just because a document exists today, does not mean it must continue to exist. *Take a zero-based approach* to existing documents.

- *Step 2: Review related documents:* the Standard, the quality manual, and other related documents.
- *Step 3: Identify the champion.* Each document (or, in the case of the quality manual, each section) should be assigned to a person who has sufficient knowledge (preferably expertise) on the subject of the document. Being the champion does not mean that he or she does all the work. But the champion is the person who coordinates the efforts of the "doers" in reviewing and adapting the document.
- *Step 4: Identify team members.* These are the "doers": the people who are actually doing the work you are documenting. They know best how the work is done. They are also the ones who will be obliged to work in a way that is consistent with the document you write. They will be audited as to how well they are complying with the document. So they must buy into it. The best way to get that buy-in is to involve them, from the start, in the process of creating the document.

PITFALL

The biggest mistake you can make in drafting quality system documents is to leave the process owners/subject matter experts out of the process. By doing that you lose their expertise and deny them ownership of what is, in fact, their process.

- *Step 5: Edit the document.* With information you obtain from the "doers," adapt the document so that it fits your organization. If there are practices in your organization that have to change, as a result of this process, document them with a Corrective Action Request (Question 72).
- *Step 6: Identify reference documents.* If specific reference documents or forms are needed to carry out the activity—or if other quality system documents are relevant—list them.
- *Step 7: Identify quality records.* If the activity generates a quality record, as defined or required by the Standard, list here the record's name, location, and owner.
- *Step 8: Get feedback from the team.* Give the draft to the team you identified above. Have them read it, mark it up, and give it back to you. (It's very wise to give them a firm deadline for response!)

Encourage them to be wholly honest. Is the document accurate? Is it workable? Can it be simpler? Does it need changes? How can we make it better?

OPPORTUNITY

It's okay to obtain the services of a professional (consultant, technical writer, etc.) to help with the drafting of the documents. But the *content* must come from the process owners and must be signed off by them as well.

- *Step 9: Create second draft.* Using the feedback obtained in Step 8, create a second draft.
- *Step 10: Have a "dry run" done.* Give the document to the "doers" (the people who are obligated to follow it). Have them review it again. Have them work with it for a few days, under actual operating conditions. This is a more reality-based review process than the simple "read and edit" chore they carried out in Step 6. Have them write down any thoughts they have on the document, and return it by a specified date.
- *Step 11: Create publication draft.* With the responses obtained in Step 10, create a publication draft. This is the draft that will be issued in accordance with your document control procedure.

At this point you may think your job is done. But it is not. In fact, no quality system document is ever really done, not even the quality manual. They are living documents, subject to change, update, and improvement as time passes and conditions change.

82. What about writing documents from scratch? Are there any special steps?

CAPSULE ANSWER

Many of the steps for creating documents from scratch are the same as those for adapting existing documents.

Hopefully, with the quality manual, you will have an existing document upon which to model your own. But this may not be the case. And, with Standard Operating Procedures (SOPs), it almost surely will not be the case. SOPs tend to be much more operation-specific than quality manuals.

If you do not have a model to adapt, then you will have to create the document from scratch. This is not entirely a bad thing. Some people find the "from-scratch" process easier than adapting existing documents (Question 81).

This method is specifically for SOPs, but it works just as well for quality manuals and work instructions.

- *First, do Steps 1–4 from Question 81:*
  - — Step 1: Decide if the document really has to exist.
  - — Step 2: Review related documents.
  - — Step 3: Identify the champion.
  - — Step 4: Identify team members.

OPPORTUNITY

Be sure to identify and document *the best practices.* The sources for these are the process owners (subject matter experts).

- *Step 5A: Identify process or processes.* The typical SOP may map out just one process. (For example, Control of Quality Records can be outlined as one process.) A work instruction is almost always just one process—or a sequence of tasks within a process. But some SOPs may cover more than one process. Your task here is to identify, by name, the process(es) that your document will describe.
- *Step 5B: Define input and output.* For each process you identified in 5A, define the input (or starting point) of the activity, and the output (or result, or ending point) of the process.
- *Step 5C: Define the action steps.* Between input and output, there are action steps that take place in order to convert the input into the output. List those action steps in sequence. For each action step, document, as required:
  - — Owner (name of function that does the work).
  - — Whether a decision is required and, if so, what the criteria are.

- Equipment and materials needed (most especially for work instructions).
- Special skills needed, if any.
- Whether inspection or some other verification is needed. If so, specify the workmanship standards or other acceptance criteria.
- Whether the step is failure prone or especially critical to meeting customers' quality requirements. If this is the case, more detail and precision may be needed to assure strict consistency.

■ *Step 5D: Create the initial draft.* Do not belabor this. Your job is not to "get it perfect" (for one thing, there is no way to do that). Your job is not even to get it right. Your job is to *get it down*—on paper, and then into the hands of the "doers" for review and feedback.

■ *Complete Steps 6–10 from Question 82:*
  - Step 6: Identify reference documents.
  - Step 7: Identify quality records.
  - Step 8: Get feedback from the team.
  - Step 9: Create second draft.
  - Step 10: Have a "dry run" done.
  - Step 11: Create publication draft.

Remember: the job is not yet "done." The document job is never really done. Each is a living document. Each remains current to prevailing practice.

Besides—and this is the really depressing news—even though you have gotten the help of the people who really do the work, there are still, no doubt, serious "bugs" in the documents. People who review the quality manual, SOPs, and so on at this stage do not really focus on them terribly well. They usually do not get around to this until much later—when the internal auditing process starts. An impending audit has a marvelous way of getting people to focus on the accuracy of procedures!

But at least you have something reasonably accurate and workable to start with. From this point on, keeping the documents current is up to the people who are obliged to follow them.

83. What about "canned" ISO 9000 documents on disk? Does it make sense to start with those?

CAPSULE ANSWER

Canned ISO 9000 document systems can cut out some of the work in creating and controlling the documents. But, as with everything, there are a few catches.

They can be very expensive. They can save you some of the scut work of keyboarding, reduce the need for some basic decision making, and give you a place to start. And they can help automate the document control process. But invest in them with care.

Many organizations—some large, most very small—are marketing ISO 9000 documents on disk. Some of these are just text files with templates of quality manuals and procedures. Others include full-blown document control systems that are compatible with various types of PC networking programs. (Some are full on-line ISO 9000 systems that automate/network many of the other subprocesses, such as corrective/preventive action and internal audits.) The idea here is to give you a head start with the documentation phase of your ISO 9000 program, and at heart the idea is good.

But often such programs are not sold on that limited premise. Their proponents tend to over-promise. Some go so far as to imply that you can simply plug the program in, crank out the documents, and voila! You've taken a very large short-cut to registration—a short-cut that more than justifies the price.

Well, maybe. Or maybe not.

There is nothing wrong with automating the process of creating and controlling ISO 9000 documents. The more of that you can do—without overburdening your implementation program—the better. One large multinational put its quality policy manual online, on both its mainframe and its Computer Aided Design (CAD) system, on a read-only basis. That saved a lot of paper circulation. It did not eliminate it entirely. And it did not help much with the subordinate documents (Standard Operating Procedures and work instructions).

And, as explained in Question 81, there is nothing wrong with adapting your ISO 9000 documents from existing documents. These can be documents of your own, or documents provided to you by others. But such documents are only a place to start. In this business, there is no such thing as "one size fits all." There is no such thing as "plug and play," whatever the salesperson says. You still have to do the work. You have to:

■ Read and understand exactly what the document says.
■ Identify parts that may not apply to your organization.
■ Identify statements that do not fit the way your organization works.
■ Amend the documents so that they:
— Fit the way your organization operates.
— Use your organization's own special language.
■ Review the result for compliance to the ISO 9000 standard.

What about the document control issue? Do these programs really help cut out some of the paper chase? Certainly, if your organization already has the computer infrastructure to support it. Check out the program's system requirements carefully. Do you have the appropriate hardware and supporting software? Is all of that well-implemented already? Is the equipment strategically placed so that everyone who needs access to the ISO 9000 documents already has access to a screen—and the training to use it?

Some of these vendors offer consulting help to go with the software, to aid you in adapting their documents to your own needs. That is great, but check out the quality of the consulting help carefully (Question 90).

The bottom line: There is no such thing as a free lunch. Effective implementation is hard work—hard work that must be done. Use whatever tools you can find that will help you. But do so with open eyes.

84. When our documents are done, then what?

Capsule Answer

Finishing the documents is certainly a milestone—but the documents are never really finished. And this is when the real work begins.

Done? Who said anything about done? You may think the documents are done. But they are not.

The sad facts of the matter are these.

In principle, *the ISO 9000 documentation job is never finished.* Remember: This is a living system. It must fit what you do, the way you do it. It must, therefore, adapt to change. Your processes undergo constant change, as a result of:

■ Customer requirements.
■ Corrective actions.
■ Preventive actions.
■ Employee suggestions.
■ Continuous improvement activities.
■ Data analysis.
■ Process changes.
■ Strategic changes in your organization.

As those changes occur, the documents must change also. (This is what makes document control so much fun. It is also what makes the document control element (Question 18) a leading source of noncompliances during internal and external audits.)

The other fact is this: *No matter how thorough you have been in developing the documents, they are probably only 70 percent "right."*

What? you ask. If we go through all the steps in Questions 81 and 82—and involve all the "doers" in the process of making these documents—why in the world would they not be right?

PITFALL

In writing documents, people sometimes lapse into "perfect world" mode or problem-solving mode—rather than documenting the process as it actually is, warts and all.

Simple. Many of the "doers" have not really focused on the details in the documents. They skim them and scan them, nod and toss them back at you, and go on to the next thing. They do not yet fully appreciate that they will be audited against the documents. Only then do they really focus on what the documents say. And then the changes come thick and fast.

That usually happens when the internal audit process starts (Question 85). By the time of registration audit, the vast majority of your quality system documents will be in their second, third, or fourth revisions. In the meantime, there are several things you should do to drive the implementation process:

■ *Carry out orientation training.* As described in Question 79, it is essential that line managers, supervisors, and leaders sit down with their people and review the relevant (and *only* the relevant) SOPs and work instructions with them. Get their feedback. Encourage them to suggest changes.

■ *Talk up the system.* Make employees understand what is happening here.
— "This is not just a fad or a phase."
— "We work to this system now."
— "We will be audited to make sure we do."
— "You have a role, you can influence it, but this is not just for now, it is for good."

■ *Stress that the ISO 9000 system is not meant to stifle initiative or innovation.* We follow the system, but we are also required to improve the system. Management needs to communicate two messages here, and communicate them consistently:
— "What does the procedure say? Are we following it?"
— "Does the procedure reflect the best practice? How can we improve the system?"

■ Make the documents a focus of problem-solving activities. When a nonconformity occurs—a customer complaint, product defect, whatever—and you are looking for the root cause, find out first if the documented procedure was followed.
— If the procedure was followed, and the nonconformity occurred, the system is flawed. (The great majority of quality problems are not people problems, but *system problems.*) How should the system and its procedure be changed?
— If the procedure was not followed, why not? Should it be changed? Would additional training solve the problem?
— If there was no procedure covering the activity, should we implement one? (Be careful here. Addressing problems simply by writing documents is what leads to the dreaded "document bloat.")

In other words, work the system. Every day. All the time. And see to it that your people do, also.

85. What's the best way to set up our internal audit program?

CAPSULE ANSWER

Your audit team must be multilevel, cross-functional, pro-active, and effectively trained.

If there is a single secret to successful implementation, it is a good strong internal audit program. Timing is important, too. You want your audit team to be trained and ready to go, just about exactly at the time the first Standard Operating Procedures (SOPs) are written, approved, and issued.

To make sure that your audit program contributes as it should to the implementation process, take great care in selecting, training, and initiating your internal auditors.

SELECTING THE AUDIT TEAM

The Standard says that audits must be done by "other than those that performed the work being audited" (Question 68). This is restrictive, but not overly so. There are many ways to structure an audit team without violating this rule. So how should you go about it?

There are many different schemes for structuring your internal audit team. Some organizations have appointed people to be dedicated, full-time internal auditors. But this smacks of the confrontational "Inspector Gadget" approach that is, for the most part, in the past, and should stay there. Other organizations have gone so far as to hire outsiders to do their internal audits for them. Despite the pretty glaring contradiction—there is more than a slight technical difference between "internal" and "external"—some registrars have actually approved this approach.

But having the audits done by *your own employees* is key to successful implementation. Properly selected, the internal audit team becomes a band of "ambassadors" of the quality system to the rest of the organization. They carry the torch, spread the word, teach, become authorities on the subject. For those reasons, the ideal profile for the internal audit team is this:

- *Multilevel.* Some organizations more or less automatically assume that internal auditors have to be management or supervisory people. This is not true. It is also not desirable. To appoint only managers or supervisors to be internal auditors is to say to the workforce: "ISO 9000 is a management system—us against you." This is the exact wrong message. The system belongs to everyone.
- *Multifunction.* Some organizations more or less automatically assume that internal auditors must be "office" people—sales, engineering, or human resources types. This is also not true, and is also not desirable. Warehouse, production, maintenance people can, and have, made excellent internal auditors. So appoint at least one representative from each function of the organization to the internal audit team.
- *Pro-active.* Every manager worth his or her salt knows the difference between an employee who is there for the check, and an employee who is interested in the job, the organization, and the future. Make sure the internal auditor candidates fit the latter profile.

Internal auditing is not rocket science. No high amount of education is required. The auditors need to be able to read and write, ask reasonably intelligent questions, follow through, and manage themselves.

While making your selection, also put out the word that anyone who would like to volunteer for internal audit duty is welcome. This will help you find people who are otherwise qualified and interested, but have perhaps been overlooked.

A common question is this: How many people should we have on our internal audit team? The rule of thumb that has worked in many places is that you should train about 10 percent of your head count as internal auditors. This tends to produce a team that is large enough to handle the audit load comfortably. It also provides for extras in case people drop out.

Another common question is: "Do we need to have a certified "lead auditor" on staff? The answer is emphatically *No*. Lead auditor training—the most misplaced, overly hyped, greed-driven training on the market today—is intended for full-time professional auditors. A good internal auditor training course covers all the same subjects (since good courses are always based on the ISO Standard 10011)—it just costs less money and takes less time.

TRAINING THE INTERNAL AUDIT TEAM

Like all other employees, internal auditors must have appropriate training. Many training programs are available.

The typical program runs two or three days, and is based on the ISO 10011 "Guidelines for Auditing Quality Systems." The best courses spend time also on the human relations aspects of internal auditing. They stress, again and again, that the audit program must never become confrontational. Audits must be thorough and persistent, but also fair, objective, and impartial. And audit findings—both positive and negative—must be supported by objective evidence.

A typical outline for a two-day internal audit course looks like this:

ISO 9000 Requirements
    Internal Auditing
        Importance of internal auditing
        Purpose of internal auditing
        Principles of effective internal auditing
    The 7 Phases of an Internal audit
        Phase 1: Audit Preparation: Scheduling and Checklists
            Evidence
            Guidelines for Preparing Checklists
        Phase 2: Opening Meeting
        Phase 3: Gather Information and Evidence
            The Effective Auditor
            Auditee Tactics
        Phase 4: Handling Suspected Noncompliances
        Phase 5: Rationalize Findings
            Types of Findings

Phase 6: Document Findings
Phase 7: Closing Meeting
Follow-up

INITIATING INTERNAL AUDITORS

OPPORTUNITY

After the practice audit, it's a good idea to debrief auditors and auditees as a group—a sort of "lessons-learned" session.

The final phase of training should be positioned as a practice audit. Group your auditors in pairs. Assign each a procedure to audit. Do this the day after training ends. Have them go through all the steps of the audit. Then convene the entire team to meet and review the results.

Once your entire team has completed a practice audit, they are ready to audit "for real."

86. How can we maximize the effectiveness of our internal audit program?

CAPSULE ANSWER

Effective internal auditing is a matter of prudent scheduling, nonconfrontational tone, thorough documentation of findings, and appropriate follow-up.

Internal auditing is one of the four reinforcement mechanisms of ISO 9000—the functions of the system that keep it active, contributing, and improving. The other three are the management reviews required by the Standard (Question 31); the surveillance audits carried out usually semi-annually by your registration body (Question 97), and the results of measurement and analysis (Question 63). The internal audits are very important:

- They are management's window into the quality system. They give management an objective, evidence-supported view of the status and effectiveness of the quality system.
- They educate employees (auditors as well as auditees) about the quality system and the functioning of the organization.
- They drive the implementation process. Most employees do not just drop the way they are doing things and hurl themselves into the arms of the ISO 9000 system. Many are indifferent at best. Some are downright skeptical. Internal audits are evidence to them, over time, that the system is real, important, and here to stay.

It is important that the internal audit system be as effective as possible. How can you assure this? For one thing, select your audit team with care. As discussed in more detail in Question 85, it is best that your audit team represent a good cross-section of levels and functions of the organization. Do not restrict the audit team to "quality people only" or "just supervisors."

Here are some other ideas for maximizing the effectiveness of your internal audit program.

SCHEDULING

You are required to audit all the processes and procedures implemented as part of your ISO 9000 system. That is a fairly large pie to divide up. You do not want each individual audit to drag on for a long, long time. That cuts into the lives not only of the auditees, but also the auditors. On average, each audit should take no more than 8 hours for the two-person audit team, from preparation and data gathering through reporting. What is the best way to set up the audit schedule? You can arrange it by:

- Clause of the Standard (7.1, 7.5, etc.).
- Area (department) of the organization.
- Procedure.

When you audit by clause, each audit may cover one or more procedures. Each audit will also cover, potentially, more than one area of the organization. That can be a lot of ground to cover.

OPPORTUNITY

Keep your audit team fresh by appointing and training new auditors from time to time.

When you audit by area or department, you most likely will be auditing more than one procedure or clause of the Standard at a time. You will find that, for some departments, such as production, you may have to cover several large procedures. This once again can result in very lengthy audits—taking up lots of time for both auditor and auditee.

Probably the most practical approach is to arrange your audit schedule first by procedure. This divides the system up into fairly digestible chunks. Some procedures cover more than one department or area of the organization. So those audits may take longer, even on a sampling basis.

When you audit this way, be sure to include, in the scope of all audits, the aspects of your system that are *not* covered by procedures but that affect the entire organization. It's a good idea to include these items on a general checklist that auditors would follow through on all audits.

Section	Description	Question
4	Quality management system—How effectively it is implemented, maintained, improved	13
5.4	Policy—Understood and implemented	26
5.6.2.	QMS—Responsibility and authority—Defined and documented	29
5.6.5	QMS—Quality manual—Available and current	20

You must audit the entire system at least once before registration. So from D-Day on—the period referred to as "Crunch Time"—your operation will be auditing intensively. This is good both for auditors and auditees. For auditors it is good training. For auditees it is good practice. Plus, and even more important, it teaches them about the system the way nothing else can.

Once you are registered, you should, at a bare minimum, audit the entire system at least once per year. Twice tends to be the norm. Three times is not unheard of and is recommended for the first year or two, until your system is mature and reaches "steady state."

You will need to audit "problem areas" more often than others. The Standard requires that the audit schedule be driven in part by audit results, which only makes sense. Registration assessors check for this.

EFFECTIVE AUDIT PRACTICES

■ Publish the schedule well in advance. It is a good idea to schedule audits for "the week of" rather than for any particular day. Then let the audit team and the auditees establish the day and time that fits their schedules best. But you must take care to enforce the schedule. Do not let it slip. Once it gets behind, it is very hard to catch up. And letting it slip sets a bad precedent.

■ While an audit team is new, let it audit the same area a couple of times. Then, start to rotate audit teams among different areas of the system. It is an error to let the same team audit the same area over a long period of time. Inevitably, objectivity starts to suffer.

PITFALL

Stress from the start that auditing is not *additional* to one's job; it is *part* of one's job.

■ Middle management can sometimes be a problem. As the segment of the management team that is under the most pressure—or at least perceives itself that way—middle managers sometimes resent the time they must devote to being audited. They also resent the time it takes for their employees to do audits. Be alert to this and deal with it directly, during the initial stages of the implementation.

■ Auditing must never become an adversarial process. Some of this cannot be avoided. But when it occurs, it needs to be addressed and eliminated.

■ In large part, it is up to the auditors—not the auditees—to set the tone. They must approach their work with an attitude of fair, objective persistence. Ban the following terms from auditors' lexicon:

— Writing you up.
— Deficiencies.
— Violations.
— Pass/fail.

■ Be sure that auditors audit not only compliance with the system (the usual objective) but also effectiveness of the system. This requires some thought and insight, especially at the reporting stage.
■ Make sure the auditors support their findings with documented, objective evidence. This is as important for positive findings as for negative ones. Failing to gather objective evidence on a consistent basis can result in noncompliances from registration assessors. Even worse, it can, over time, erode the credibility of the findings and, therefore, of the program itself.

FOLLOW-THROUGH

■ Handle internal audit noncompliances as part of your corrective action system (documented in your procedure under Corrective Action).
■ From time to time, analyze audit results by department and by clause of the standard. Report these analyses at Management Reviews. This gives you solid evidence of "effectiveness of the system."
■ When an area of the system (either a department, or a quality system function) turns up chronic noncompliances:
— Follow up on corrective actions with follow-up audits, carried out by the same audit team.
— Increase the frequency of audits, at least in the short term.
— Highlight these issues at management review meetings.

GENERAL

Your audit team is a valuable asset to your organization. They are performing an essential service. It is vital that they be recognized for this.

■ Hold regular meetings so that they can air their experiences.
■ Consider treating them to lunch or dinner several times a year, as a way of thanking them.

87. What are some of the common perils and pitfalls to successful implementation?

CAPSULE ANSWER

In the end, successful implementation requires an approach that is persistent and pro-active, rather than defensive and resentful.

Just as every organization is different, so is every implementation. But there are some common pitfalls that you should do your best to avoid.

- *Implementing "from the bottom up."* It is surprising how often this one happens. Sometimes, top management is direct about it— "leave us out until the very end." Even more insidious is the senior management group that appears to be involved, but is not. The rest of the workforce reads this loud and clear, and it can add months to the implementation process. *Top management must lead and drive the process, consistently and persistently.*
- *Trying to do "just enough to get registered."* Some organizations say, "let's just do ISO 9000 for Process A and B, or Plant D and E. Because those are the plants shipping to the customer yelling at us about ISO." Such half measures are, in the end, self-defeating. Going about things this way eats up time and resources. Successful ISO 9000 implementation spans the entire organization. It brings everyone in.
- *The Lone Ranger syndrome.* Project champions, such as Management Representatives, sometimes take too much of the work upon themselves. Successful MRs learn to delegate, by selling, cheerleading, wheedling, and cajoling if necessary. Getting implemented and getting registered requires 100 percent effort by *all* concerned. Everyone will share in the benefits, so everyone should share in the pain.
- *Getting carried away with documentation.* ISO 9000 is, in part, about documentation. But another key to success is creating only as much documentation as is necessary to meet the Standard—plus documentation felt to be meaningful and value-added. Projects have been torpedoed by paperwork bloat. Be ruthless and vigilant about it. Make every document earn its keep. Keep documents short.

- *Springing the system on the workforce all at once.* ISO 9000 is not a state secret. Its success in large part depends on the acceptance and involvement of everyone in the organization whose work affects quality. Plan your implementation with ongoing awareness sessions (Question 79). This way, as the project gains momentum, people find themselves working with it instead of around it.
- *Failure by champions to become educated in the requirements.* No one claims that reading the ISO 9000 requirements is fun. It can be more like undergoing root canal work, or parsing the IRS code. But there is no substitute—not this book, not any other book—for reading them and understanding them. You cannot learn the requirements with one read-through. You can't even learn them by studying them for hours on end. Learning the requirements requires repeated exposure.
- *Regarding the ISO 9000 system as separate from the rest of the business.* It will seem this way at first. But part of effective implementation is making the system "part of how things work" rather than "this program we have to do for some customer." The successful, contributing ISO 9000 system—that is a benefit, rather than an expense—is one that becomes transparent within the organization.
- *Considering the work "done."* Some organizations get implemented, and get registered, and go "Whew! Thank goodness that's over—now we can go back to doing things the way we used to!" Big mistake. A ISO 9000 system is not a "thing" that you can put your arms around. It is a constantly evolving process, an evolution, a way of doing business that changes and adapts as your business must change and adapt in order to survive.

88. How can we tell if our ISO 9000 system is really working?

CAPSULE ANSWER

You can tell the ISO 9000 system is really working when employees at all levels use it and follow it as a matter of course.

When it becomes not just tolerated, but accepted. And not just accepted, but an automatic, reflexive part of "the way we do things here."

The term for this is *transparency*. When your ISO 9000 system is really working, it is transparent in your organization.

But (surprise, surprise) this does not happen overnight. It usually does not even happen prior to registration. Up to that point, and beyond, the ISO 9000 system is new, different, intrusive. It forces people to change their ways, most in small ways, some in large. People resent this, as they tend to resent all change. Some resist, at least passively. Others ignore it and hope that it will go away. Some become "maliciously obedient," hewing to the "letter of the law" but doing no more unless and until confronted.

They can run, but they cannot hide. Once the internal audit process starts, employees are confronted with the quality system, and their obligations under it, on a regular basis. Most elect to join 'em, having failed to beat 'em. And that is the big turning point.

CAUTION

Unfortunately, some organizations never reach the transparency stage. These organizations implement "for the certificate only," "to get the customer off our back." They do the minimum needed to get registered. They allot meager resources to implementation and maintenance. They communicate to their employees, by word and deed, that, lip service notwithstanding, "this is just a big joke and it really doesn't matter." Which makes their ISO 9000 system a cost, rather than a benefit. And that is a shame.

Once the euphoria of registration has passed, and the organization has a couple of successful surveillance assessments under its belt, the ISO 9000 process starts to become transparent. Here are some definitive clues that this is happening:

- Virtually no major noncompliances are written during internal audits. When the program first starts, internal audits will routinely turn up quantities of majors. A few may still slip through, even after registration. By the time you reach transparency, majors tend to be a thing of the past.
- Middle managers and line employees are routinely writing corrective action requests. This is a strong sign because the typical middle manager has tended to address problems on a solo basis rather

than working through the system. When middle managers begin working through the system, it is a sign that they (finally) see value and merit in it.

■ Management reviews become strategic in nature rather than tactical. The first few management reviews are extremely tactical, do-it-by-rote exercises. Later, after implementation and registration, senior management tends to realize what an excellent tool these reviews are not only for reviewing the quality system processes, but for improving the process over the long term.

■ Employees watch the numbers. With your system, you track performance against defined goals, and every procedure has goals, objectives, and "improvement" built in. A wise management communicates the "score" to employees on a regular basis. You know you are at a state of transparency when employees keep an eye on the numbers themselves.

■ Procedures and other quality system documents are routinely being reviewed and updated as processes change and improvements are put into place. Up until transparency, documents tend to lag behind changes—sometimes for a long time—and are not caught except by internal audits. When transparency sets in, people automatically take care of the documents that pertain to their jobs. They want them to be right.

89. Once safely registered, how can we best capitalize on our ISO 9000 system?

CAPSULE ANSWER

Make your ISO 9000 system an active, visible part of your business and its image, not just internally, but also externally.

In time, you will find that your ISO 9000 quality system is its own reward. This presumes, of course, that you do the following:

■ Implement the system fully (no shortcuts, half measures, corner cuts, or other funny business).
■ Operate it in that manner on an ongoing basis.

ISO 9000 registration will reward you by allowing you to do these things:

- Retain the business of key customers (often the main reason organizations get into ISO 9000).
- Compete effectively with others who are also registered. (This could give you an edge in competing for business based in the European Union.)
- Acquire new business from other customers who require (or prefer) ISO 9000 registration.

OPPORTUNITY

Another way to capitalize on your ISO 9000 system is to optimize its benefits by making it absolutely central to the operation of your organization.

But there are other things you can do to capitalize on your registration:

- Make press announcements in all publications that serve your marketplace. Be sure to stress the benefits of ISO 9000 registration and the implications it will have for your business worldwide.
- Use your registration logo on business cards, letterhead, brochures, annual reports, and marketing materials.
- Promote your registration status within industry trade groups.
- Prepare briefings for key customer accounts. Even now, despite the determined efforts of various writers and consultants, knowledge of ISO 9000 is fairly limited. So be sure to explain what ISO 9000 is in some detail. More important, stress to your accounts the benefits of doing business with a firm whose quality system is registered.
- Make ISO 9000 a major component of sales presentation materials. When going after new accounts, let your quality message rest on your ISO 9000 registration.
- Publicize your quality system success stories to all appropriate stakeholders of your business.
- Encourage your suppliers to register to the Standard:
  — Audit your key (critical) suppliers against the ISO 9000 requirements.
  — Offer them training, briefings, orientation in the requirements.

As one of the ISO 9000 guidance documents states:

Mutually advantageous partnership arrangements between purchaser and supplier (can supplement) third-party audits. Such partnerships focus on mutual efforts toward continuous quality improvement, and the use of innovative quality technology. In instances where purchaser/supplier partnerships are fully developed, third-party certification often plays an important early role. (This) may become relatively less important as the partnership develops, and progresses beyond the requirements of the (ISO 9000) standards.

90. Should we hire a consultant to help us implement our ISO 9000 system?

> ### CAPSULE ANSWER
>
> It is not necessary—or necessarily desirable—to hire a consultant to help you implement ISO 9000. But if you do, be sure to hire a good one.

Not necessarily. In the long run, the most effective way to implement it is to do it yourself, without outside help. The process of trial and error, trial and error results in a system that is truly unique to your organization, fully owned by all levels and functions.

There is just one catch. The trial-and-error method takes a long time. If you are up against a customer deadline, you may not have time to waste. Trial and error cost money, too. Cost conscious organizations want to get from "A" to "B" by the shortest possible (and most cost-effective) route.

So some organizations choose to hire consultants to help them implement their ISO 9000 systems. There are two valid reasons to consider this:

■ A qualified consultant helps shorten the time it takes to get the job done.
■ A qualified consultant aims to help you develop a quality system to improve performance (rather than simply "going for registration")—thereby adding value rather than simply acting as a cost.

A good consultant can help you get the "job" done faster. He or she does this by using experience, creativity, and hard work to plan a system that fits your organization and your needs while avoiding excess effort and mistakes. What a good consultant has to offer is *options*—lots and lots of options.

Although there is no evidence to support this, experience suggests that a reasonably priced consultant who knows his or her organization, and who works hard and conscientiously, will save your organization money compared with the trial-and-error approach. He or she should most certainly reduce the level of misery and frustration. If he or she is any good.

So what makes a good consultant?

- *Criterion 1: Direct, hands-on, and repeated ISO 9000 experience.* No substitute. A good consultant is one who has personally supervised ISO 9000 implementation not just once, but many times, from start to finish. This is no job for academics, self-promoters, or 90-day wonders. You want scars.
- *Criterion 2: Eclectic experience.* A good consultant can still be highly effective even if he or she does not have personal experience in your industry. But he or she should have experience in a wide range of industry sectors and organization sizes. All other things being equal, if you are choosing between two consultants who meet Criterion 1, and one has personal experience in your industry and the other one does not, choose the former.
- *Criterion 3: Eclectic work experience.* Some consultants have spent their whole careers as quality managers, or engineers, or in some other fairly narrow discipline. This is not a bad thing, in and of itself. But give a slight edge to a consultant who has worked in several areas of business.
- *Criterion 4: Hands-on work ethic.* Consultants can be divided into two general categories: those who talk and those who do. You want the latter. A good consultant is not content to sit in a conference room all day, dispensing pearls of wisdom to the top brass. A good consultant deals not only with senior management, but also with the troops. He or she gets to know all the players. He or she is with the doers, or out on the floor, training, writing or editing documents, cheerleading, cajoling, solving problems, moving the process along, constantly striving not only to implement the system, but to improve it.

- *Criterion 5: Strong people skills.* A good consultant is comfortable and effective dealing with people at all levels and functions of the organization. While it would be pleasant if he or she were universally liked, this is not a requirement. But the consultant must command respect and attention, even if (as is sometimes the case) the organization elects not to heed his or her advice in certain instances.

- *Criterion 6: Practical and down to earth.* Every consultant has a general (and, preferably, effective) approach to the situation. A good consultant is practical, experienced, and flexible enough to adapt his or her approach to fit each client's situation and meet each client's needs precisely. A good consultant never forgets whose system it really is. Would you like to know the sure sign of a consultant who has not a clue as to what he or she is talking about? When he or she is blindly and arrogantly adamant that the client change to fit *his* system. This is the "my way or the highway" route. Avoid it.

- *Criterion 7: Good personal fit.* Organizations are as different, and as individualistic, as people. By all means, pick a consultant with whom you are personally comfortable. You will be working with the person for a pretty intense and lengthy stretch of time. It will not always be pleasant. And it does not have to be. All it has to be is effective.

- *Criterion 8: Client-first philosophy.* A good consultant is conservative on interpretation of the Standard and works hard to help you avoid noncompliances. Still, a good consultant strives to help you develop a QMS that fits *your* organization and its structure, style, and objectives—rather than making "auditability" the primary consideration.

- *Criterion 9: Strives to work him or herself out of a job.* A good consultant intends to leave you with a system that you know, understand, and are comfortable with—so that you do not have to pay him or her in perpetuity.

91. What is the one key thing we can do to make our system work better for us?

CAPSULE ANSWER

Set one or more aggressive quality/customer related goals and aim the ISO 9000 system (and the entire organization) at meeting that goal.

A well-implemented, contributing ISO 9000 system is more than just a "certificate on the wall." It is a system for improving organization performance.

Ultimately, what you must always do in order to survive as an organization is to meet your customers' needs. Your ability to do that drives everything else: whether or not you make money, how well you compete, how fast and large you grow.

Your ISO 9000 system is a blueprint for helping you improve your organization's ability to meet customer needs. You can optimize it—not just today but in the years to come—by doing the following:

■ Identify a specific need that is high (if not at the top) on the list of your most important customers. Customers have many needs, and there is always the temptation to clutter up this process by grabbing too many. Narrow it down to just one. It could be something like:
  — On time delivery.
  — Fast turnaround time for orders.
  — Low variability around target values for critical characteristics.
  — Absence of visual defects.
  — Fast installation.
■ Develop a way to measure your performance at meeting this need.
  — On time delivery can be measured as the days (or hours) elapsed between required delivery time and actual delivery time.
  — Turnaround time can be measured as the number of days (or hours or weeks) elapsed between order receipt and order shipment.
  — Variability can be tracked using Statistical Process Control or other statistical methods.
  — Visual defects can be measured by comparing product to defined standards each of which has a numerical value.
  — Installation time can be measured as the number of days (or hours) elapsed between delivery and full operation of the product.
■ Using that measurement method, identify your performance level now (baseline). Resist the temptation to exclude certain products or transactions, or to impose certain caveats that complicate the measurement process and cast doubt upon its objectivity. In other words, don't cheat.

OPPORTUNITY

The best way to keep the system growing, improving, and contributing is for management to consistently and persistently walk the talk. That imperative never goes away.

■ Set a specific target or goal for your performance. Do not make it easy. And do not make it simply "aggressive." Make it borderline impossible (at least as people perceive it today).

■ Update your quality policy statement (Question 26) to include the new target as your "objective for quality."

■ Educate the entire workforce, consistently and persistently, on the customer need and the goal. Encourage them to think about how their own job performance affects the organization's ability to improve its ability to meet the customer need. Ask for their help, on an ongoing basis, in improving the organization's ability to reach the goal.

■ Take the customer need and the goal into account during all critical quality system activities:
— Establishment of process measurements.
— Analysis of data for improvement.
— Management reviews.
— Organization planning.
— Analysis of corrective and preventive action.

■ Using the measurement method, publicize the organization's "score," very visibly, at frequent intervals. Track trends also.

When you reach your goal—which you will, if your ISO 9000 system and organization team is aimed at achieving it—set the goal higher still. Or re-evaluate customer needs and set a brand new goal. Always keep the system reaching for something. You can always do better and ISO 9000 can be your system for making it so.

PART FOUR

Registration—and After

Registration is *the* imprimatur on your quality management system—at least as far as the outside world is concerned. It's also quite a milestone. Achieving it gives your organization a unique feeling of satisfaction.

Registration, as you'll read in this section, is not the be-all and the end-all. It is, in a sense, like a driver's license. When a person gets his or her first driver's license, this does not signify that the person is an expert driver. All it signifies is that the person has been checked by an objective authority and found to have the basic/minimal skills needed to be licensed to drive.

So it is with registration: It signifies that your quality system meets the ISO 9001 requirements and that all the systems are in place. As time goes on and you undergo surveillance assessments, it *tends* to signify that your system is getting better, stronger, more effective. Here the evidence is not so strong. Many organizations have kept registration without any noticeable improvement.

Registration is not, then, the best indicator of the health of your quality system. That is better shown by the state of the internal measurements that you set for yourself, tracking how you're doing against the objectives that most matter to you.

This section tells all about registration. What it is, how it works, what's involved, and how to get there.

92. What are the general requirements for registration to ISO 9000?

CAPSULE ANSWER

To register to ISO 9000, you must meet all the requirements applicable to your location, pass an audit by a registrar, and undergo scheduled surveillance assessments.

Basically, any organization may register to ISO 9000. It matters not what your product or service is, or the size of your organization, or where you are located.

To register to ISO 9000, you must:

- Implement a system that meets all the requirements in ISO 9000: 2000. You may, by virtue of the "permissible exclusions" clause (Question 14), omit requirements that are not relevant to your process. Reduction in scope is restricted to the requirements in Section 7 (Product and Service Realization) and includes processes such as:
  - Design/Development (Questions 43–49) for organizations that are not design responsible
  - Customer property (Question 60 for organizations that do not have or use property owned by customers
- Operate the system for three, and preferably six, months.
- Complete at least one cycle of internal audits (Question 68).
- Undergo an audit of your organization by a registrar, most preferably an accredited one (Question 93) and, where mandated, one that is approved by your customer(s).
- Resolve and close out all noncompliances raised by the audit.
- Undergo surveillance assessments at defined intervals (usually every six months), and close out noncompliances raised by those assessments as required by the registrar.
- Follow the registrar's rules as spelled out in your registration agreement.
- Pay your bills.

93. How should we choose our ISO 9000 registrar?

> ## CAPSULE ANSWER
>
> Obtain bids and presentations from a number of registrars—and do not let price be the sole criterion.

With thorough research, thought, and analysis. Your ISO 9000 registrar is no ordinary vendor. Its employees become privy to the inner workings of your organization. They're around for at least three years (the term of the normal registration contract). You might as well pick someone that is not only qualified, but is also someone you won't mind seeing come through your door!

You have dozens and dozens from whom to choose. There are close to 60 quality system registrars operating in the United States as of late 1999. Others, knowing a growing market when they see one, are entering the business every day. So how do you choose? Shop price and go for it?

Well, not exactly. Price is certainly a factor. But there are several others that experience shows are just as important, if not more so. When evaluating potential registrars, consider the following:

■ *Compatibility.* Registration bodies are organizations. Every organization has its own culture, language, demeanor, "feel." Some are relatively relaxed and easygoing. Others are stuffy, bureaucratic, incommunicative. Some bend over backward to hold their customers' hands. Others have a remarkable ability to make the registration process more difficult than it needs to be.

  — When narrowing your selection, interview at least one person (preferably an actual auditor, not just a "business development" person) by phone or in person. Size them up. Judge for yourself how good the "fit" is between your organization's culture and theirs.

  — You may pick up gossip to the effect that certain registrars are "easier" in audits than others. Do not let this affect your selection process. First of all, it most likely is not true. And even if it is, you don't want an "easy" registrar. You want a fair, objective, rigorous assessment, initially and ongoing. Otherwise, you are not getting your money's worth.

— By all means, pick the registrar whose culture is the most compatible with yours. After all, you are going to be "married" to the registrar for at least the first three years.

OPPORTUNITY

If your firm does business overseas as well as in North America, you may want to choose a registrar that is accredited not only by the U.S. group (Registrar Accreditation Board), but also by one of the international accreditation bodies.

■ *Name recognition.* Some of the registrars on the list have "household" names, at least in the consumer sense. Underwriters Laboratories is probably the best example. Lloyd's Register Quality Assurance would be if it were the same as, or related to, Lloyd's of London, which it is not. KPMG (formerly Peat Marwick) is familiar. Name recognition in the general public sense is not terribly critical. What's important is that the name means something to your customer(s). When selecting a registrar, think beyond your needs today. Think ahead.

— If you are doing business overseas, or plan to, poll your customers and/or prospects. Get an idea from them about the registration bodies they are familiar with. Lean toward a registrar that has name recognition in the areas, and among the market sectors, with which you do business, or plan to do business. This may mean selecting a registrar that is accredited not just by RAB (a U.S. accreditation body), but also by one of the overseas bodies (UKAS, RvA, etc.).

■ *Location.* Increasingly, registrars have North American-based operations. Some even have multiple branches around the country. This has benefitted the customer base, which saves on travel costs. Even so, location is still an issue. The farther away your registrar (and, even more important, the audit team), the higher your costs. (And please don't be unduly swayed by registrars that "include" travel expenses in their quotations. The cost is still in there.)

— When evaluating registrars, find out where their assessors are based. Some may employ field people who work out of their homes, very close to you. Others may bring people in from a great distance. Wherever they're from, you'll pay the cost of getting them to you and back, and these costs are not necessarily foreseeable.

■ *Cost.* This is an important factor. Some clients do not realize that there is no set fee or expense structure for quality system registrars. Though the number of "audit days" to quote is more or less "standardized" by the code of practice that accredited registrars must follow, the process is otherwise totally market driven. So the costs, for the same facility, can swing wildly among five or six different registrars!

— Obtain specific and detailed quotation from a number of registrar candidates. (Six is a good number.) Make sure each quotation includes at least the following:
  ■ Daily rate for assessment (registration and surveillance).
  ■ Estimated number of days for registration assessment.
  ■ Estimated number of days for surveillance assessment.
  ■ Expenses reimbursable by you.
  ■ Location of assessor(s).
  ■ Cost of registration renewal (if any).
  ■ Cost of document review.
  ■ Cost of certificates (some charge for extra ones).
  ■ Cost of additional accreditations (usually the first one, for example, RAB, is free; others may cost additional).
  ■ Administrative fees.
  ■ Application fees.
  ■ Other fees.

— Line up and analyze the overall expense, including everything, *over the first three years of the relationship* (the typical length of a "registration").

— Pay special attention to the registrars' policies on travel expenses. Some actually charge for travel *time* as well as expense.

— Does the registrar carry out a complete systems re-audit to "renew" your certificate? Most do. Some do not. This is a major cost factor to consider as well. (Although, typically, the savings is not as much as one might think.)

— Reduce all the quotation to a single number per registrar, and compare.

■ *Relevant experience.* How much experience does the registrar have in your particular field? Accreditation includes some presumption of experience. And each audit team is required to have at least one member with "relevant experience" in your core business area. But it's a good idea to select a registrar that has actually registered organizations in your particular market niche. More experience and better understanding of your process and market tend to result in more effective audit results for you. It also makes audits more efficient. Your people will not have to spend quite as much time "educating" the assessors.

94. What steps does the typical registration process include?

CAPSULE ANSWER

Although practices may vary slightly among registrars, the registration process itself is well-defined and takes place in a series of steps.

The registration process is fairly well-defined and somewhat consistent among registrars. Still, there is some variation in practice from registrar to registrar. They are, after all, independent entities. They are free to set their own policies, as long as their policies, as interpreted by their accreditation body, meet the relevant requirements. So the process described here is fairly generic. For the specifics pertaining to your situation, see a registration body or confer with a qualified consultant.

■ *Step 1: Implement ISO 9000.* But of course you're going to implement ISO 9000 first! Isn't that obvious? Maybe it is. But the key thing here is, your system must be fully implemented and up and running for a minimum of three, and preferably six, months prior to the registration audit. This is the amount of time it takes to build up the amount of evidence, records, and so on that assessors expect to see.

    For details on implementation, see Questions 74–91. In capsule form, implementation means:

  — All required elements of ISO 9000 are in operation.

  — At least one complete cycle of internal audits (Question 68) has been completed.

— At least one management review (Question 31) has been completed. (You should have completed many more than one—it's
recommended that you hold one management review per
month during the implementation phase.)
— Corrective and preventive action activity (Questions 72–73)
is ongoing.

■ *Step 2: Select your registration body* (Question 93). Begin this process while implementation is going on. You want to have your registrar selected, on board, and scheduled no later than three
months prior to your target registration date. (Registrar schedules
vary; some may need more lead time than that, depending on
market conditions.) You also need time to learn and digest your
particular registrar's policies and procedures.

PITFALL

There are registrars that structure themselves to offer both consultancy
and registration—skirting the prohibition against this. Be very wary.

— Most registrars offer general training in ISO 9000. This can
be helpful.
— Your registrar will also answer questions about interpreting
the Standard. This too can be helpful.
— If you have multiple sites, coupled perhaps with some "reduction in scope" situations (Question 14), the registrar can answer questions about how to structure your system. This can
be very helpful.
— But registrars are not allowed to "consult." They will not tell
you how to implement your system. They will not tell you how
to fix what's wrong, or how to develop systems that will meet
the requirements.

■ *Step 3: Obtain a pre-assessment (Readiness Review).* This is an op-
tional step, and it costs money. But it is highly recommended.

A pre-assessment is a sort of "practice audit." Its results do
not "count." Its scope usually does not include your entire quality
system. You and the registrar determine what will be audited and
how long that audit will take.

What is the point? A pre-assessment gives your people a taste
for what an ISO 9000 audit is like. (Very important. Those that
have been through other supplier audits may think they know

what's coming—but odds are they do not.) It gives you some feedback on how your system is doing, so that you can "fine tune" it before the registration audit:

— Unlike the registration audit, for a pre-assessment you can usually direct the registrar to the areas that you want covered. *ALWAYS* have them assess the parts of your system about which you are the *LEAST* confident. Otherwise, you are not getting your money's worth.

— In addition to the above, *ALWAYS* make sure the pre-assessment covers the following areas of your system:

■ Management review
■ Corrective and preventive action
■ Internal audit

■ *Step 4: Undergo the desktop study of your quality system.* This may happen prior to preassessment. It depends on your registrar's policies. And the specific documents can vary from registrar to registrar, too. Some only want your Quality Manual (Tier 1) (Question 20) in advance. Some want to see your Standard Operating Procedures (Tier 2) (Question 18) also. And some will not want to see these documents "off site." Instead they will review them as the first part of the On-Site Assessment (see Step 5).

Regardless, virtually every registrar does what is often called a "desktop study" of your quality system. This means that they review at least your Quality Manual. They compare it with the requirements of ISO 9000: 2000. They assess it to make sure that the Quality Manual complies with the requirements.

If you have done a thorough and conscientious job of developing your quality system, the desktop study should pose no problems. You will always get a comment or two, a niggle here and there. Odds are the registrar will find at least one important issue for you to address. Address the issues either by changing the documents or explaining your position to your registrar. (By the way, do not hesitate to stand up for your system and "defend" it vigorously. The registrar's role is to fairly assess compliance with the requirements, not to tell you how to run your organization.)

■ *Step 5: Undergo the on-site audit.* This is where the rubber meets the road. White knuckle time. The registrar's audit team shows up on the appointed day, checklists in hand. If they did the desktop study in advance, they have already determined that your quality system, as documented in your Quality Manual, conforms to the

OPPORTUNITY

Always escort registration auditors as they work. Write down everything they say. The ideal escorts are members of your internal audit team. And it's good experience for them.

Standard. Now they want to see if you are actually doing what the manual and related documents say you are doing.

The audit team usually consists of two or more people, depending on the size of the facility and the scope of the process:

— Lead auditor, who handles relations between the audit team and the auditee personnel. This person plans the audit, supervises the auditors, and takes the lead on interpreting the Standard and audit results.

— One or more additional auditors. These are qualified people but usually somewhat less experienced. The audit team must always include someone with "relevant" industry experience. Most registrars try to include a person whose experience in your field is even more specific than that.

The auditors, following a predetermined plan and checklist, audit your system (Question 95). At the end, they give you a verbal report of their findings. Included, in writing, are any noncompliances that they have found, with supporting evidence (Question 96).

■ *Step 6: Correct and close out noncompliances.* All major noncompliances reported during registration audit must be closed out before registration can be issued. You are not permitted to say or claim that you passed or got registered until all majors are corrected, closed out, and confirmed by the registration body. Sometimes, the registrar will require on-site verification that the noncompliance is fixed. Other noncompliances may be closed out via the submission, review, and approval of revised documents or procedures.

Minor noncompliances must be resolved, also. But usually, the registrar will report them to you and agree to review your corrective action at the first surveillance assessment. In the meantime, you are considered registered.

■ *Step 7: Registration and the certificate.* Registration is conferred when the registrar issues its certificate of registration to you (and not until then). This includes the scope of registration, which spells out exactly what processes and locations are covered by the registration.

So now you're registered! Are you done? Is it time to relax? Can things go back to "the way they were before?" See Question 97.

95. What is the typical ISO 9000 registration audit like?

> ### Capsule Answer
>
> Assessors do a thorough, fair, and objective job of assessing your system to evaluate its compliance with ISO 9000 requirements. But going through the process is seldom fun.

How about stressful? Nerve-wracking? White-knuckle time? Well, it can be all of that. Even if you are very well prepared—even if you have been through many other kinds of audits—an ISO 9000 registration audit can be one long Maalox moment.

First, let us differentiate between an ISO 9000 registration audit and the typical supplier quality assurance audit to which many ISO 9000 candidates have been exposed in the past.

The difference is simple. In the typical supplier quality assurance audit, the auditors spent the majority of their time in the conference room, reading reports and looking at charts and talking to the quality manager, quality engineer, and other management and quality types. ISO 9000 auditors spent most of their time in the work place, where the process of "product/service realization" happens. They are out on the factory floor, in the showroom, in the sales offices, in the purchasing department—everywhere. They want to see not just what you claim, on paper, is going on. They want to see what is *really* going on.

Scary, huh?

THE PRELIMINARIES

Usually, before coming to your site, the ISO 9000 auditors do a desktop study of your quality system. They review your Quality Manual (Level 1) and, sometimes, your Level 2 documents (Standard Operating Procedures). They provide a report of their findings. If there are compliance problems, you are, as a rule, required to correct them by the time of the registration audit.

Also, in advance, the audit team provides you with a schedule and plan for the registration audit. The plan is not etched in stone. Findings as the audit progresses can influence the schedule. But it gives you a feel as to what they are going to cover, and when.

When the auditors arrive at your site, they begin with a brief meeting with management. They discuss the audit schedule and scope and answer any questions that may arise.

GATHERING DATA

The audit team usually starts with a quick walking tour of the site, to get oriented. Then, as written in their schedule, they fan out across your site, escorted by your designated guides. These, by the way, should be members of your internal audit team. It is good experience for them. But it is not the guides' job to answer questions or direct the audit team. The guides' role is to get the assessor access to departments, people, and records.

Assessors visit virtually every department of your organization. They work off checklists—some of them generic (specific to the requirements of ISO 9000: 2000), as well as checklists specially created for your audit. Their job is to assess the effective implementation of your ISO 9000 system and assure themselves that there are no noncompliances with the ISO 9000 requirements. No area, no employee, no function of the organization is off limits.

Registration assessors:

- *Question employees.* They ask about the quality policy, request explanations of their duties, question them about their training.
- *Observe activities.* Always, they are comparing what they see with what the quality system says about the quality practices. Are they real? Are they in place? Are they being followed consistently? Are they effective?
- *Check records.* This is the most objective form of evidence, to support findings of compliance as well as noncompliance.

But they do all this on a sampling basis. There is no way, even with the amount of time allotted, to cover any particular activity with complete depth. So assessors sample across activities, employees, and records.

Once they have satisfied themselves that the area in question is in compliance, they document evidence of that fact and move on promptly. They do not engage in fishing expeditions. And they are not in the business of digging, digging, digging until they find something wrong. They audit for compliance, not for noncompliance.

If they find, or suspect, that there is a noncompliance, they pursue the matter until they have gathered sufficient evidence one way or the other. And they will almost always alert the escort to the possibility of a noncompliance.

How should you deal with an assessor? Conventional wisdom says that you should not volunteer anything. Just answer the questions. If you want to be that way, fine. But this creates an adversarial atmosphere where there really should not be one. It anticipates that the assessor is "out to get you." They are not. (Well, a tiny handful may be. But usually the registrars promote these characters into management sooner or later.) You want your system to be fairly and thoroughly audited. For that reason, it is smart, in the long run, to be as open and honest with the assessor as possible.

Should you argue with the assessor? By all means. Assessors will often ask "devil's advocate" questions. They often challenge the many judgment calls that you inevitably make while implementing your system. The worst mistake you can make is to bow your head and meekly accept an implied criticism or challenge to your system. Stand up and defend it.

If you have done your homework, understand the requirements of the Standard, and have made a good faith effort to comply, the assessor has no choice but to take into account the unique workings of your organization and situation in making his or her judgment. This does not mean that an assessor has the power to waive the requirements. But the assessor is supposed to do a fair, balanced, and objective job of interpreting the requirements in light of your organization. The assessor can only do that when you explain the decisions you have made.

If the assessor has you cold, there's only one thing you can do: Swallow hard, own up, and go on to the next thing.

What the assessor will not do—must not do—is give you advice or direction about your system. That is consultancy, and consultancy is forbidden. Assessors are limited to evaluating the system and its compliance with the requirements. They are not allowed to tell you how to fix what may be wrong.

> ## OPPORTUNITY
>
> Do not hesitate to ask assessors questions as they work. You can learn much about the ISO 9000 Standard and process by doing this.

Periodically, during the audit, the assessment team will meet privately to review their findings and revise their schedule. They may revisit an area or function once or twice. Sometimes they will also schedule interim meetings with management to brief them on their findings.

But most of that is reserved for the final phase of the assessment.

THE GOOD NEWS, THE BAD NEWS

When the data-gathering phase has ended, the assessment team meets to compile their findings. They strive to compile positive as well as negative findings. But the negative findings are the most important, and they do a thorough job of identifying these and documenting them with objective evidence.

Most registrars rank noncompliances as major or minor (Question 96). They also present opportunities for improvement. These are sometimes called observations.

At the closing meeting, the assessment team presents their findings. If there are no "majors," the audit team will tell you so immediately, and tell you they are recommending you for registration.

They will also report any noncompliances. These are documented on noncompliance reports. You are virtually certain to have some noncompliances. You may have as few as half a dozen, you may have as many as 80. However many you have, you must close out the majors before registration can be conferred—and you must close out all others by the time of the first surveillance assessment.

Keep in mind there is no real way to fail. Even a major or two is not failing. The only way to fail is to refuse to fix a major noncompliance documented and raised by the assessors.

96. What happens if the assessors find noncompliances in our system?

CAPSULE ANSWER

Nonconformities are a fact of life. Since they represent an opportunity to improve, view them positively—even if a major noncompliance delays registration for a time.

Relax. The auditors will find noncompliances (sometimes called nonconformities or deficiencies or opportunities). They always do. It is not the end of the world. Unless you get a major and refuse to correct it, you cannot fail. The worst thing that can happen is that your registration will be delayed until you fix whatever problems are found.

ISO 9000 assessors are trained to do a very thorough job of documenting their findings with objective evidence. Before they reach a conclusion, they gather as many facts as they can. To do this, they mention the possibility of noncompliances whenever they find them during the audit. This is to give you and your people a chance to respond and explain.

Please do not hesitate to do so. Please do not hesitate to defend your system whenever it is challenged. Sometimes assessors challenge something just to play devil's advocate. But usually it is because they need additional information. They only want to render judgment that is fair and supported by evidence. They can only get the facts from you. The worst thing you can do, when an auditor challenges something during an audit, is to bow your head and swallow hard and meekly defer. (Well, that isn't the worst thing you can do. The worst thing you can do is say, "To heck with that requirement.")

There is another thing to consider. Every organization is different. The Standard, prescriptive though it is, has a lot of "wiggle room." There is a certain amount of latitude in many areas as to how you can comply. In implementing your system, you make dozens of judgment calls. You can count on assessors to probe those judgment calls and judge for themselves how well your system meets the intent of the requirements. So your people need to understand how the ISO 9000 system works in their particular area. There is no substitute for this!

After gathering their data, the assessors retire for a time to put together their findings. They write some sort of nonconformity reports (the nomenclature varies among registrars), and prepare a verbal briefing of their findings.

Then, at the *closing meeting*, the audit team presents a verbal report of its findings. (They follow this up with a written report later.) The report includes a list of nonconformities supported by documentary evidence. If the team is doing its job, there will be no surprises at this meeting. They will have pointed out potential nonconformities to audit guides during the audit itself. They do this mainly to confirm that they understand what they are seeing. Even if the auditee implements an immediate corrective action, the observation is still noted for the report.

There are five generic types of findings a registration assessor may raise. (The nomenclature may vary among registrars.)

- *Compliance*—the assessed area meets the requirements.
- *Strengths and weaknesses*—Assessors are expected to comment on these.
- *Major noncompliance*
  - Absence of compliance to an ISO 9000 requirement (i.e., no system in place to address the requirement).
  - Total breakdown of a system intended to meet the requirement (i.e., system exists but does not work).
  - Any noncompliance that could result in the furnishing of a nonconforming product or service to a customer.
  - Any noncompliance that could either reduce the usability of the product/service for their intended purpose, or result in their failure to do so.
  - Any noncompliance that, in the assessor's judgment, could result either in the failure of the quality system to assure controlled processes and products, or to materially reduce its ability to do so.
  - A number of minor noncompliances against one requirement (constitutes a total breakdown of the system).
- *Minor noncompliance*
  - A failure in some part of the system related to an ISO 9000 requirement (that does not fit any of the definitions under major).
  - A single observed lapse in one area of the quality system.
- *Observation*
  - Opportunity for improvement; potential/emerging noncompliance.

Just one major noncompliance will delay your registration. You will be required to implement corrective action, and have its effectiveness verified by the registrar, before registration is conferred. The time frame here can vary, but is often on the order of 90 days. Some majors require a return visit by the auditors for close-out. Others can be closed out via documents, confirmed at the first surveillance assessment. This is at the discretion of the audit team. They will thoroughly brief you on all this at the closing meeting.

Most often, what assessors will raise will be one or more minor noncompliances. A reasonably small number of these (say, less than 8 or so), liberally dispersed in the system, will not hold up registration. Each is reported on a noncompliance form, and you're normally given until the first surveillance assessment to resolve them.

The audit team specifically does *not* give advice about how to fix nonconformities. This would be consultancy, and registration bodies are barred from offering consultancy to clients. They will often give you the benefit of their judgment, however. If you pose the question: "If I do XYZ, will that take care of the noncompliance," the auditors will usually say Yes or No.

The audit report will include commentary on the perceived strengths and weakness of the system. It will also present a (sometimes sizable) list of opportunities for improvement. These are not as actionable as noncompliances, but they are not just for show, either. You should consider them and act upon them when it makes sense to do so. Otherwise you're not getting your money's worth.

97. What must we do to keep ISO 9000 registration?

Capsule Answer

Surviving surveillance assessments takes consistent, persistent work on an ongoing basis—not just during the week leading up to the audit.

Two things. Deal effectively with the outcomes of the surveillance assessments, and pay your registrar's invoices.

Of these, the invoices are the easiest to deal with. The surveillance assessments are another matter.

At prescribed intervals, often every six months or so, the registrar re-assesses a part of your ISO 9000 system. You always know when they are coming—this is arranged in advance. What you do not necessarily know is the part of your system that they plan to re-assess (although some registration bodies disclose this information, too). They will tell you that when they walk in the door. As with registration audits, your entire system is an open book. So you have to be on your toes!

You must resolve any noncompliances that arise from surveillance assessments in an agreed amount of time, and they must be closed out by the registrar. Otherwise you put your registration in jeopardy.

What are the factors that make surveillance assessments such a challenge?

FACTOR 1: THE INFAMOUS "LET-DOWN" SYNDROME

Once an organization has become registered, a "let-down" syndrome often kicks in. "We made it!" goes the theory. "Now we can kick back." But you cannot. You must keep working your system. You will be amazed how fast that first six months goes by—and there they are, the assessors again, knocking on your door, poised to re-assess part of your ISO 9000 system.

If you have faithfully and conscientiously worked your system, no problem. If you have not, you can be in real trouble. It is a lot easier simply to work your system, day by day, than it is to recover from the trauma of a nasty surveillance assessment.

It is like taking care of a swimming pool. If you do 5 or 10 minutes of work every day, it is easy to keep the water clear and clean. But you have to do that 5 or 10 minutes of work every single day. If you do not, then you get to do 2 or 3 days worth of work to clear your pool of all that lovely lime Jell-O.

FACTOR 2: IT DOESN'T GET EASIER (AT LEAST IT SHOULDN'T)

In some ways, your registration audit is among the easiest you will ever undergo. Surveillance audits (when what we're talking about are the really *good* registrars) tend to get tougher, pickier, more specific.

Why? Registrars get to know your firm and your process. They dig deeper and more persistently. They want to see that your system and process is improving. That is the whole point of the thing.

Surveillance assessments are one of the four "reinforcement mechanisms" of ISO 9000 (Question 11). But they are more than that. They are tangible evidence that your system is here to stay, as long as you want to stay registered.

PART FIVE

ISO 9001: 2000
Making the Transition

The ISO 9000 family of standards was first published in 1987. In 1994, it underwent a relatively light revision. The structure and order of the requirements were left undisturbed. Some minor wording changes were made. Key additions included quality planning, data control, maintenance, and preventive action. Those changes don't seem particularly major. But for many registered organizations, even these relatively light changes were headaches.

The 2000 round of changes is much more drastic. This revision leaves relatively *little* of the 1994 Standard undisturbed. In addition to the complete re-ordering of the requirements (into process sequence), the scope of coverage has expanded significantly. Even so the length of the Standard has actually gone down. It is 18 percent shorter than the 1994 version, and the number of "shalls" has decreased by nearly 4 percent.

Overall, though, the revisions are major improvements. Some language muddiness has been removed. Most of the widget-making manufacturing orientation is gone. There is strong focus on process management, on understanding and meeting customer needs, and (most significantly) on improvement—of product/service, process, and the quality system. The Standard is, if anything, even more flexible and generic than before.

ISO states that organizations need not completely rewrite and re-structure their existing quality systems to mirror ISO 9001: 2000. That's good. For organizations with functional, registered quality systems that conform to ISO 900X: 1994, complete rewriting and restructuring would not be a value-added activity. There are, however, some new subprocesses and subsystems that must be added (Question 99). There are quite a few changes in existing systems to be made (Question 100). Some requirements have actually become less strict and/or prescriptive, and an organization may adjust its system to conform to this if it wants to.

In this part we present guidelines for organizations currently operating quality systems consistent with ISO 900X: 1994. An assumption is that the QMS to be upgraded fully complies with the requirements and is well implemented. We have tried to make these guidelines as efficient as possible, while taking care to address *all* of the additions and changes prescribed by the new Standard.

Remember: The guidelines in this section *are no substitute* for reading and understanding the actual text of the Standard, and thoughtfully applying it to your particular circumstances.

98. What is the overall nature of the changes to the Standard?

CAPSULE ANSWER

The new Standard is a dramatic rewriting and restructuring of the 1994 version—and it is a major improvement.

ISO 9001: 2000 is a virtually complete rewrite of the 1994 Standard. On the whole, the revision is excellent. For one thing, virtually all instances of muddiness that were so maddening in the 1994 Standard are gone. Certain "implicit" requirements, always inferred but difficult for English-speaking people to discern in the 1994 standard, are now explicit. The new structure makes more intuitive sense. It fairly well matches the generic process flow of a typical organization—whether manufacturing or service-oriented.

Certain important themes have been added or reinforced in the new Standard. There is strong emphasis on understanding and meeting customer needs. There are new requirements concerning process design and improvement. Arguably the most important addition is the intensified emphasis on measurement, analysis of data, and use of that data to improve the ability of the process to meet customer needs.

Other changes include:

- The requirements have been completely reordered into a more or less process orientation.
- Fifteen new requirements have been added (Question 99).
- Twenty-eight requirements have undergone various degrees of tightening/change (Question 100).
- The distinction among ISO 9001/2/3 has been removed; a new "permissible exclusions" clause (Question 14) permits you to render "not applicable" clauses from Section 7 (Realization of Product/Service) that are not relevant to your organization and its processes.
- Element 4.10 (Inspection and Testing) has undergone a serious meltdown; the requirements are really no less strict, only a lot less prescriptive and specific.
- Element 4.12 (Inspection and Test Status) no longer appears as a stand alone requirement. It has been subsumed in the Product Identification and Traceability requirement (Question 59).
- Element 4.19 (Servicing) no longer appears as a standalone requirement. It has been subsumed in the product/service realization requirements in Section 7 (Questions 50, 57).

To stay registered, you need to transition your system to meet the revised requirements. You need not, however, go back to the drawing board. You can maintain the existing structure of your implemented, registered quality system and still comfortably meet the revised requirements.

As to timing, check with your registration body. If the 1994 experience is any guide, registration bodies publish schedules and advisories well in advance of the audits that they will certainly carry out to check transition status. Schedule your transition process with plenty of time to allow for a full round of internal auditing of the revamped system as well as corrective action and follow-through.

99. What are the new requirements in the Standard?

Capsule Answer

There are 15 new requirements in the Standard. You need to address these in your quality policy manual and also, in many cases, by writing new procedures.

There are 15 separate and distinct requirements that did not appear in ISO 900X: 1994. It is necessary to address these requirements in your quality system.

You must address all of these in your quality policy manual (Question 20). It is not necessary, though, to rewrite or restructure your Quality Manual. You need to edit it.

- To each section, add cross-referencing to the clause/paragraph numbers of ISO 9001: 2000. The table on page 259 guides you in this.
- To each of the quality manual sections referenced in the following table, add policy language describing your policies with respect to the new requirements. You can find the details on what is required in the question listed in the last column.

Please note our suggestion that you create a new "Section 21" in your quality manual. Here you will address a body of new requirements for data, measurement, and improvement.

You may also need to create Standard Operating Procedures (SOPs) for certain of the new requirements. Again, you can find guidance in this in the questions listed in the last column.

ISO 9001 Clause		ISO 9001: 2000 Title	See
1994	2000		Question
4.1.2.2	6.3	Facilities	36
4.1.2.2	6.4	Resources—Work environment	38
4.1	5.1	General requirements	23
4.1	5.2	Customer focus	24
4.2	0.4	Compatibility with other management systems	16
4.2.3	5.4.1	Planning—Quality objectives	27
4.2	5.5.4	QMS internal communication	19
4.2	1.2	Permissible exclusions	14
4.3	7.2.3	Customer related processes—Customer communication	51
4.3	7.2.1	Customer related processes—Identification of customer requirements	52
4.9	7.1	Planning of realization processes	50
4.21*	8.5.1	Planning for continual improvement	71
4.21*	8.2.1	Measurement of customer satisfaction	65
4.21*	8.2.3	Measurement and monitoring of processes	41
4.21*	8.4	Analysis of data	70

*No equivalent in ISO 900X: 1994.

100. What existing requirements have been tightened/ strengthened?

CAPSULE ANSWER

About 28 requirements have been tightened/strengthened, and your new system needs to address these.

There are 28 existing requirements that have been tightened and/or strengthened. You must address these changes in your quality manual (by updating the policy language). You will also need to address them in the procedures that you already have that relate to these requirements.

The table on page 260 lists the 1994 requirements that have been tightened/strengthened. For full details on the specifics of the changes, see the questions listed in the last column.

ISO 9001 Clause		ISO 9001: 2000 Title	See Question
1994	2000		
1.0	1.0	Quality system requirements—Scope—General	13
4.1.1	5.3	Quality policy	26
4.1.2.2	6.1	Resource management—General requirements	32
4.1.2.3	5.5.3	QMS—Management representative	30
4.1.3	5.6	Management review	31
4.2.1	4.1	Quality management system requirements	17
4.2.1	5.5.5	QMS—Quality manual	20
4.2.3	5.4.2	Planning—Quality planning	28
4.3c	7.2.2	Customer related processes—Review of customer requirements	53
4.4.4	7.3.2	Design and/or development inputs	44
4.4.5	7.3.3	Design and/or development outputs	45
4.4.6	7.3.4	Design and/or development review	46
4.4.8	7.3.6	Design and/or development validation	48
4.4.9	7.3.7	Control of design and/or development changes	49
4.6.1 4.6.2	7.4.1	Purchasing control	54
4.7	7.5.3	Production and service operations—Customer property	60
4.9	7.5.5	Production and service operations—Validation of processes	40
4.11a	7.6	Control of measuring and monitoring devices	62
4.12	7.5.2	Production and service operations—Identification and traceability	59
4.13	8.3	Nonconformity review and disposition	69
4.14.1	8.5.2	Corrective action	72
4.14.3	8.5.3	Preventive action	73
4.15	7.5.4	Preservation of product	61
4.17	8.2.2	Internal audit	68
4.18	6.2.1	Human resources—Assignment of personnel	33
4.18	6.2.2	Human resources—Training, awareness, and competency	34
4.19	7.1	Planning of realization processes	50
4.20	8.1.2	Measurement and analysis	64

101. Are there any 1994 requirements that were not changed or made more demanding?

CAPSULE ANSWER

Eleven of the 1994 requirements, though reworded, do not present additional requirements or strictness. Even so, it is wise to review them.

Yes. Virtually all the requirements were rewritten. But for 11 of them, the rewriting does not add strictness. In fact, in some cases, the rewording renders the requirements more general and, perhaps, easier to comply with, depending on your situation.

Once you have addressed the new requirements (Question 99) and the changes listed in the accompanying table, you should take a look at the remaining requirements from 1994. These requirements have all been reworded, some extensively. But a careful review suggests that the changes are for the most part neutral and should not affect your compliance status. You are, therefore, free to amend your system, or not, as you see fit.

ISO 9001 Clause			See
1994	2000	ISO 9001: 2000 Title	Question
4.1.2.1	5.5.2	QMS—Responsibility and authority	29
4.2.2a 4.2.2b	4.2	General documentation requirements	18
4.4.1 4.4.2 4.4.3	7.3.1	Design and/or development—General requirements	43
4.4.7	7.3.5	Design and/or development verification	47
4.5	5.5.6	QMS—Control of documents	21
4.6.3	7.4.2	Purchasing information	55
4.6.4	7.4.3	Verification of purchased product	56
4.8 4.12	7.5.2	Production and service operations—Identification and traceability	59
4.9 4.19	7.5.1	Operations control	57
4.10	8.2.4	Measurement and monitoring of product	58
4.16	5.5.7	QMS—Control of quality records	22

Appendix: Cross-Reference Tables

ISO 900X (1994) to ISO 9001: 2000

ISO 9001: 1994		ISO 9001: 2000			
Clause	Title	Clause	Title	Question
4.1	Management responsibility	5.1	General requirements	23
4.1.1	Management responsibility—Quality policy	5.3	Quality policy	26
4.1.2.1	Organization—Responsibility and authority	5.5.2	QMS—Responsibility and authority	29
4.1.2.2	Resources	6.1	Resource management—General requirements	32
		6.3	Facilities	36
		6.4	Resources—Work environment	38
4.1.2.3	Management representative	5.5.3	QMS—Management representative	30
4.1.3	Management review	5.6	Management review	31
4.2.1	Quality system	4.1	Quality management system requirements	17
		5.5.5	QMS—Quality manual	20
4.2.2a 4.2.2b	Quality system—Procedures	4.2	General documentation requirements	18
4.2.3	Quality system—Quality planning	5.4.1	Planning—Quality objectives	27
		5.4.2	Planning—Quality planning	28
4.3	Contract review	7.2.2	Customer related processes—Review of customer requirements	53
4.4.1	Design control—General	73.1	Design and/or development—General requirements	43
4.4.2	Design and/or development planning			
4.4.3	Organizational and technical interfaces			
4.4.4	Design control—Design input	7.3.2	Design and/or development inputs	44
4.4.5	Design output	7.3.3	Design and/or development outputs	45

(Continued)

ISO 9001: 1994		ISO 9001: 2000		Question
Clause	Title	Clause	Title	
4.4.6	Design review	7.3.4	Design and/or development review	46
4.4.7	Design verification	7.3.5	Design and/or development verification	47
4.4.8	Design validation	7.3.6	Design and/or development validation	48
4.4.9	Design changes	7.3.7	Control of design and/or development changes	49
4.5	Document and data control	5.5.6	QMS—Control of documents	21
4.6.1	Purchasing—General	7.4.1	Purchasing control	54
4.6.2	Purchasing—Evaluation of subcontractors			
4.6.3	Purchasing data	7.4.2	Purchasing information	55
4.6.4	Verification of purchased product	7.4.3	Verification of purchased product	56
4.7	Control of customer supplied product	7.5.3	Production and service operations—Customer property	60
4.8	Product identification and traceability	7.5.2	Production and service operations—Identification and traceability	59
4.9	Process control—Special processes	7.5.5	Production and service operations—Validation of processes	40
4.9	Process control—General	7.1	Planning of realization processes	50
		7.5.1	Operations control	57
4.10	Inspection and testing	8.2.4	Measurement and monitoring of product	58
4.11	Control of inspection, measuring, and test equipment	7.6	Control of measuring and monitoring devices	62
4.12	Inspection and test status	7.5.2	Production and service operations—Identification and traceability	59
4.13	Review and disposition of nonconforming product	8.3	Nonconformity review and disposition	69

(continued)

(Continued)

| ISO 9001: 1994 | | ISO 9001: 2000 | | |
Clause	Title	Clause	Title	Question
4.14.2	Corrective and preventive action	8.5.2	Corrective action	72
4.14.3	Preventive action	8.5.3	Preventive action	73
4.15	Handling, package, storage, preservation, and delivery	7.5.4	Preservation of product	61
4.16	Control of quality records	5.5.7	QMS—Control of quality records	22
4.17	Internal quality audits	8.2.2	Internal audit	68
4.18	Training	6.2.1	Human resources—Assignment of personnel	33
		6.2.2	Human resources—Training, awareness, and competency	34
4.19	Servicing	7.5.1	Operations control	57
		7.1	Planning of realization processes	50
4.20	Statistical techniques	8.1.2	Planning	64

ISO 9001: 2000 to ISO 900X (1994)

ISO 9001: 1994		ISO 9001: 2000		Question
Clause	Title	Clause	Title	
1.0	Quality system requirements—Scope—General	1.0	Management responsibility	13
1.2	Permissible exclusions	—	No equivalent	14
4.1	Quality management system requirements	4.2.1	Quality system	17
4.2	General documentation requirements	4.2.2a 4.2.2b	Quality system—Procedures	18
5.1	General requirements	4.1	Management responsibility	23
5.2	Customer focus	—	No equivalent	24
5.3	Quality policy	4.1.1	Management responsibility—Quality policy	26
5.4.1	Planning—Quality objectives	4.2.3	Quality system—Quality planning	27
5.4.2	Planning—Quality planning	4.2.3	Quality system—Quality planning	28
5.5.2	QMS—Responsibility and authority	4.1.2.1	Organization—Responsibility and authority	29
5.5.3	QMS—Management representative	4.1.2.3	Management representative	30
5.5.4	Quality management system—Internal communication	—	No equivalent	19
5.5.5	QMS—Quality manual	4.2.1	Quality system—General	20
5.5.6	QMS—Control of document	4.5	Document and data control	21
5.5.7	QMS—Control of quality records	4.1.6	Control of quality records	22
5.6	Management review	4.1.3	Management review	31
6.1	Resource management—General requirements	4.1.2.2	Resources	32
6.2.1	Human resources—Assignment of personnel	4.18	Training	33

(continued)

(Continued)

ISO 9001: 1994		ISO 9001: 2000		
Clause	Title	Clause	Title	Question
6.2.2	Human resources—Training, awareness, and competency	4.18	Training	34
6.3	Facilities	—	No equivalent	36
6.4	Resources—Work environment	—	No equivalent	38
7.1	Planning of realization processes	4.9	Process control—General	50
		4.19	Servicing	50
7.2.1	Customer related processes—Identification of customer requirements	—	No equivalent	52
7.2.2	Customer related processes—Review of customer requirements	4.3	Contract review	53
7.2.3	Customer related processes—Customer communication	—	No equivalent	51
7.3.1	Design and/or development—General requirements	4.4.1	Design control—General	43
		4.4.2	Design and/or development planning	
		4.4.3	Organizational and technical interfaces	
7.3.2	Design and/or development inputs	4.4.4	Design control—Design input	44
7.3.3	Design and/or development outputs	4.4.5	Design output	45
7.3.4	Design and/or development review	4.4.6	Design review	46
7.3.5	Design and/or development verification	4.4.7	Design verification	47
7.3.6	Design and/or development validation	4.4.8	Design validation	48
7.3.7	Control of design and/or development changes	4.4.9	Design changes	49
7.4.1	Purchasing control	4.6.1	Purchasing—General	54
		4.6.2	Purchasing—Evaluation of subcontractors	

(Continued)

ISO 9001: 1994		ISO 9001: 2000		Question
Clause	Title	Clause	Title	
7.4.2	Purchasing information	4.6.3	Purchasing data	55
7.4.3	Verification of pur-chased product	4.6.4	Verification of pur-chased product	56
7.5.1	Operations control	4.19	Servicing	57
		4.9	Process control—General	57
7.5.2	Production and ser-vice operations—Identification and traceability	4.12	Inspection and test status	59
		4.08	Product identification and traceability	59
7.5.3	Production and ser-vice operations—Customer property	4.7	Control of customer supplied product	60
7.5.4	Preservation of product	4.15	Handling, package, storage, preservation, and delivery	61
7.5.5	Production and ser-vice operations—Vali-dation of processes	4.9	Process control Special processes	40
7.6	Control of measuring and monitoring devices	4.11	Control of inspection, measuring, and test equipment	62
8.1.2	Planning	4.20	Statistical techniques	64
8.2.1	Measurement of cus-tomer satisfaction	—	No equivalent	65
8.2.2	Internal audit	4.17	Internal quality audits	68
8.2.3	Measurement and monitoring of processes	—	No equivalent	41
8.2.4	Measurement and monitoring of product	4.10	Inspection and testing	58
8.3	Nonconformity re-view and disposition	4.13	Review and disposi-tion of nonconforming product	69
8.4	Analysis of data	—	No equivalent	70
8.5.1	Planning for continual improvement	—	No equivalent	71
8.5.2	Corrective action	4.14.2	Corrective action	72
8.5.3	Preventive action	4.14.3	Preventive action	73

Index